ALL ANGELS IN THE BIBLE

BY J. PITTERSON
Published by Celestial Guide Publications

Unless otherwise stated, all scripture quotations are taken from the King James Version of the Bible.

ISBN 978-1-7381632-3-6 (Paperback)
ISBN 978-1-7381632-0-5 (E-book)
ISBN 978-1-0688520-1-5 (Hardcover)

Copyright © 2023 Celestial Guide Publications

All rights reserved

Contact: j.pitterson23@gmail.com

Table of Contents

Introduction 1

Chapter 1: Angels in the Book of Genesis 6

1. Genesis 3:24 6
2. Genesis 6:1-4 6
3. Genesis 16:7-14 7
4. Genesis 18:1-22 9
5. Genesis 19:1-26 12
6. Genesis 21:15-19 16
7. Genesis 22:11-15 17
8. Genesis 24:7-40 19
9. Genesis 28:10-12 24
10. Genesis 31:11-13 25
11. Genesis 32:1-2 26
12. Genesis 48:15-16 27

Chapter 2: Angels in the Book of Exodus 28

1. Exodus 3:1-2 28
2. Exodus 14:19 29
3. Exodus 23:20-23 29
4. Exodus 25:18-22 30
5. Exodus 26:1-31 32
6. Exodus 32:34 36
7. Exodus 33:1-3 36
8. Exodus 36:8-35 37
9. Exodus 37:7-9 41

Chapter 3: Angels in the Book of Numbers 42

1. Numbers 7:89 42
2. Numbers 20:16 42
3. Numbers 22:22-35 43

Chapter 4: Angels in the Book of Judges 47

1. Judges 2:1-4 47
2. Judges 5:23 48
3. Judges 6:11-22 48
4. Judges 13:3-21 51

Chapter 5: Angels in the books of Samuel 55

1. 1 Samuel 4:2-4 55
2. 1 Samuel 29:9 56
3. 2 Samuel 6:2 56
4. 2 Samuel 14:17-20 57
5. 2 Samuel 19:27 58
6. 2 Samuel 22:11 59
7. 2 Samuel 24:16-17 59

Chapter 6: Angels in the books of Kings 61

1. 1 Kings 6:23-35 61
2. 1 Kings 7:29-36 63
3. 1 Kings 8:6-7 64
4. 1 Kings 13:18 65
5. 1 Kings 19:5-7 65
6. 2 Kings 1:3-15 66
7. 2 Kings 6:15-17 69
8. 2 Kings 19:15-19 70
9. 2 Kings 19:32-36 71

Chapter 7: Angels in the books of Chronicles 73

1. 1 Chronicles 13:6 73
2. 1 Chronicles 21:12-30 73
3. 1 Chronicles 28:18 77
4. 2 Chronicles 3:7-14 78
5. 2 Chronicles 5:7-8 80
6. 2 Chronicles 32:21 80

Chapter 8: Angels in the Book of Job.....................82

1. Job 1:6-12 82
2. Job 2:1-7... 83
3. Job 4:17-19 85

Chapter 9: Angels in the Book of Psalms 86

1. Psalm 8:4-6 86
2. Psalm 18:10 87
3. Psalm 34:7.. 87
4. Psalm 35:5-6 87
5. Psalm 68:17 88
6. Psalm 78:25 88
7. Psalm 78:49 89
8. Psalm 80:1... 89
9. Psalm 91:11 90
10. Psalm 99:1 90
11. Psalm 103:20 90
12. Psalm 104:4... 91
13. Psalm 148:2... 91

Chapter 10: Angels in the Book of Ecclesiastes 92

1. Ecclesiastes 5:6 92

Chapter 11: Angels in the Book of Isaiah.................93

1. Isaiah 6:1-6... 93
2. Isaiah 37:16 94
3. Isaiah 37:36.. 95
4. Isaiah 63:9.. 95

Chapter 12: Angels in the Book of Ezekiel..............97

1. Ezekiel 1:4-28 97
2. Ezekiel 9:1-3 101
3. Ezekiel 10:1-22 102
4. Ezekiel 11:22-23 105
5. Ezekiel 28:14-16 106

   6.   Ezekiel 41:18-25...107

Chapter 13: Angels in the Book of Daniel 109

1. Daniel 3:28 109
2. Daniel 6:22 110

Chapter 14: Angels in the Book of Hosea...............111

1. Hosea 12:4 111

Chapter 15: Angels in the Book of Zechariah........ 112

1. Zechariah 1:9-19 112
2. Zechariah 2:3-5.. 114
3. Zechariah 3:1-7..115
4. Zechariah 4:1-5 116
5. Zechariah 5:5-11...117
6. Zechariah 6:1-8 119
7. Zechariah 12:8 120

Chapter 16: Angels in the Book of Matthew..........122

1. Matthew 1:20 122
2. Matthew 1:24 122
3. Matthew 2:13-15 123
4. Matthew 2:19-21 123
5. Matthew 4:6-11 124
6. Matthew 13:39-50..125
7. Matthew 16:27 127
8. Matthew 18:10 127
9. Matthew 22:30 128
10. Matthew 24:31-36..128
11. Matthew 25:31-41 129
12. Matthew 26:53.. 131
13. Matthew 28:2-7 132

Chapter 17: Angels in the Book of Mark 134

1. Mark 1:13 134
2. Mark 8:38 134

3. Mark 12:25 135
4. Mark 13:27 135
5. Mark 13:32 135
6. Mark 16:1-7 136

Chapter 18: Angels in the Book of Luke 138

1. Luke 1:11-22 138
2. Luke 1:26-38 140
3. Luke 2:6-16 142
4. Luke 2:21 144
5. Luke 4:1-10 144
6. Luke 9:26 145
7. Luke 12:8-9 146
8. Luke 15:10 146
9. Luke 16:22 147
10. Luke 20:36 147
11. Luke 22:43 148
12. Luke 24:13-23 148

Chapter 19: Angels in the Book of John 151

1. John 1:51 151
2. John 5:4 151
3. John 12:29 152
4. John 20:11-18 153

Chapter 20: Angels in the Book of Acts 155

1. Acts 5:16-20 155
2. Acts 6:15 156
3. Acts 7:30-54 156
4. Acts 8:26-28 161
5. Acts 10:1-8 162
6. Acts 10:22 164
7. Acts 11:12-17 164
8. Acts 12:6-11 165
9. Acts 12:13-16 167
10. Acts 12:21-23 168

11.	Acts 23:8-9 169
12.	Acts 27:21-25 170

Chapter 21: Angels in the Book of Romans........... 172

1. Romans 8:38-39 172

Chapter 22: Angels in the books of Corinthians ... 173

1. 1 Corinthians 4:9 173
2. 1 Corinthians 6:1-4 173
3. 1 Corinthians 11:10 174
4. 1 Corinthians 13:1 175
5. 2 Corinthians 11:12-14 175

Chapter 23: Angels in the Book of Galatians 177

1. Galatians 1:6-8 177
2. Galatians 3:19 178
3. Galatians 4:14 178

Chapter 24: Angels in the Book of Colossians 180

1. Colossians 2:18-19 180

Chapter 25: Angels in the books of Thessalonians 181

1. 1 Thessalonians 4:15-16 181
2. 2 Thessalonians 1:6-8 182

Chapter 26: Angels in the Book of Timothy 183

1. 1 Timothy 3:14-16 183
2. 1 Timothy 5:21 184

Chapter 27: Angels in the Book of Hebrews 185

1. Hebrews 1:1-14 185
2. Hebrews 2:2-9 188
3. Hebrews 2:16 190
4. Hebrews 9:5 190
5. Hebrews 12:21-24 191
6. Hebrews 13:2 192

Chapter 28: Angels in the books of Peter 193

1. 1 Peter 1:10-12 193
2. 1 Peter 3:22 194
3. 2 Peter 2:4-11 194

Chapter 29: Angels in the Book of Jude 197

1. Jude 1:5-9 197

Chapter 30: Angels in the Book of Revelation 199

1. Revelation 1:1-2 199
2. Revelation 1:19-20 200
3. Revelation 2:1-25 200
4. Revelation 3:1-16 205
5. Revelation 5:1-3 208
6. Revelation 5:9-12 209
7. Revelation 7:1-3 210
8. Revelation 7:9-12 210
9. Revelation 8:1-13 211
10. Revelation 9:1-18 215
11. Revelation 10:1-10 218
12. Revelation 11:1-14 220
13. Revelation 11:15-19 223
14. Revelation 12:7-9 224
15. Revelation 14:6-13 225
16. Revelation 14:14-20 227
17. Revelation 15:1-8 228
18. Revelation 16:1-21 230
19. Revelation 17:1-5 234
20. Revelation 17:7-18 235
21. Revelation 18:1-3 237
22. Revelation 18:21-24 238
23. Revelation 19:9-10 239
24. Revelation 19:17-18 239
25. Revelation 20:1-3 240
26. Revelation 21:9-10 241

27. Revelation 22:1-10 244
28. Revelation 22:16 245

Conclusion 247

Introduction

Do you think it is possible to meet someone by chance, chat with them on current topics, and have the conversation become so pleasant that you invite them to dinner? Later, you realize that this person is not human but an angel! If you find my imagination a little bit overflowing, know that people like us have had such an experience and others are probably still living it today. These circumstances are not isolated in the Bible. Abraham experienced it, as did his nephew Lot and many others.

Abraham welcomed God, accompanied by two angels, into his home under the oaks of Mamre, eating, drinking, and talking with them (Genesis 18). Likewise, Lot, his nephew, welcomed two men into his home, talking, eating, and drinking with them, only to later realize that they were both angels (Genesis 19:1-16). This was the case for Gideon when he talked with the angel in his field (Judges 6:11-24). This is why the author of the Epistle to the Hebrews warns us in these terms: "Do not forget hospitality; for, in exercising it, some have entertained angels, without knowing it (Hebrews 13:2)." In the Old Testament, angelic manifestations were very common. In this text from Psalm 91:11, "For he shall give his angels charge over thee, to keep thee in all thy ways," we can understand that all those who walk with God are constantly in an angelic environment.

In the Bible, four categories of angels are clearly identified—angels, cherubim, seraphim, and archangels. The word angel appears 297 times; the word seraph appears twice; cherub is mentioned 95 times; and archangel is mentioned twice. In Latin, the word angel comes from "angelus"; in ancient Greek, it comes from "ággelos;" and the Hebrew word is "mal'akh." In all these languages, the word means "messenger." Angels can be defined as spiritual beings endowed with extraordinary powers, fulfilling the functions of messengers of God, and having the ability to travel from the spiritual world to the physical world and from the physical world to the spiritual world. They were used by God to:

- Secure the Garden of Eden (Genesis 3:24)
- Accompany and secure the people of Israel during the crossing of the desert (Exodus 14:19)
- Communicate battle strategies (Joshua 5:13-15)
- Participate in a military battle (2 Kings 19:32-35)
- Announce what was going to happen (Luke 1:13-14)
- Bring a message (Acts 10:3-6)
- Bring a plague (1 Chronicles 21:14-15)
- Perform miracles (John 5:3-4)
- Prepare food for someone (1 Kings 19:5-8)
- Motivate someone (Judges 6:12-16)

- Help a person in distress (Daniel 6:21-23)
- Protect men and women of God from danger (2 Kings 6:15-17)
- Execute God's judgment (Revelation 15:1)

Based on the number of times they are mentioned in the Bible, we can easily deduce that angels have played an important role in the history of humanity and that they probably continue to play an important role in it. If they have had so much involvement in what is happening on earth since the Garden of Eden, would it still be the same today?

This is why everyone should study angels to understand their functioning and modus operandi. If God used them throughout most of human history—from the Garden of Eden to the establishment of the early church—it would not be surprising if He continued to use them even today since angels are his messengers. Who knows? Their activities might even be increased in this end-time period!

We have been trained mentally to see angels as winged beings dressed in white and radiant garments, endowed with exceptional beauty, at least by our standards. That's not entirely the truth. We must take the time to study these beings in the light of the Bible, which allows us to dissect the true from the false, the reality according to the Scriptures from the fiction of cinema.

However, it must be admitted that studying angels in the Bible is not an easy job, and one can easily miss certain details. The facts about angels are scattered throughout the Bible and, therefore, it is easy to get lost. Hence, the preparation and publication of this work. Indeed, this book presents a list of all the biblical texts involving the action or intervention of an angel and provides a summary for each of them. It is, therefore, a tool that will help those who are interested in the subject, those who want to know more about angels, Bible teachers, Bible students, students of theology, including angelology, theologians, and those who want to go deeper their knowledge in the Word of God. You could thus see that the angels:

1. Can appear and disappear.
2. Eat, drink, and prepare food.
3. Are sociable.
4. Carry weapons when necessary.
5. Sing and play a musical instrument.
6. Do not seek to impress or attract attention.
7. Do not accept worship.
8. Manifest in various ways: luminous beings, human forms (mature men, young adolescents, etc.), frightening creatures, pillar of fire, burning bush, etc.
9. Operate in different ways:
    a. Physically, where we can see them and sometimes catch a glimpse of them
    b. Spiritually, where only certain people can see them
    c. In visions and dreams, where only the people having the visions or the dreams can see them

Some facts about angels in the Bible:

1. The Bible speaks of the myriads and myriads of angels who serve God; that is to say, they are innumerable. They will always outnumber the population of planet earth.

2. There are no female angels.

3. They never manifest as young children.

4. They are of different categories: angels, cherubim, seraphim, and archangels.

5. The Bible doesn't often give the names of angels. Only two names are communicated to us in the biblical texts: Gabriel and Michael.

6. They do not act to promote themselves to humans. They carry out their missions with the greatest discretion.

7. They are endowed with extraordinary abilities.

8. They can be scary. This is why they often say to those to whom they manifest themselves: "Fear not."

This book presents in a few words some essential elements about angels in the light of the Bible. I invite you to take a moment to delight in everything that the Word of God tells us concerning angels, as well as a specific synthesis of each text. Hoping that these writings will provide you with in-depth knowledge about the subject, I wish you a good reading.

Chapter 1
Angels in the Book of Genesis

1. **Genesis 3:24**

   So he drove out the man; and he placed at the east of the garden of Eden Cherubims, and a flaming sword which turned every way, to keep the way of the tree of life.

   Summary

   God took Adam and Eve out of the garden and placed armed cherubim, which are a class of angels, as guardians to keep people from returning to the garden and eating the fruit of the tree of life.

2. **Genesis 6:1-4**

   1 And it came to pass, when men began to multiply on the face of the earth, and daughters were born unto them,

   2 That the sons of God saw the daughters of men that they were fair; and they took them wives of all which they chose.

   3 And the Lord said, My spirit shall not always strive with man, for that he also is flesh: yet his days shall be an hundred and twenty years.

4 There were giants in the earth in those days; and also after that, when the sons of God came in unto the daughters of men, and they bare children to them, the same became mighty men which were of old, men of renown.

Summary

The phrase "the sons of God" mentioned in this passage refers to angels who developed a sexual attraction to women and forced them to have sex with them. This led to the appearance on earth of a hybrid race composed mainly of giants with superhuman abilities. They were known for their strength and prowess and were "the heroes of ancient times, men of renown." Some have called this hybrid race the "Nephilim."

In response to all this, God set the lifespan of man on earth at 120 years. The flood in Noah's time could be a consequence of these events.

3. **Genesis 16:7-14**

7 And the angel of the LORD found her by a fountain of water in the wilderness, by the fountain in the way to Shur.

8 And he said, Hagar, Sarai's maid, whence camest thou? and whither wilt thou go? And she said, I flee from the face of my mistress Sarai.

9 And the angel of the Lord said unto her, Return to thy mistress, and submit thyself under her hands.

10 And the angel of the Lord said unto her, I will multiply thy seed exceedingly, that it shall not be numbered for multitude.

11 And the angel of the Lord said unto her, Behold, thou art with child and shalt bear a son, and shalt call his name Ishmael; because the Lord hath heard thy affliction.

12 And he will be a wild man; his hand will be against every man, and every man's hand against him; and he shall dwell in the presence of all his brethren.

13 And she called the name of the Lord that spake unto her, Thou God seest me: for she said, Have I also here looked after him that seeth me?

14. Wherefore the well was called Beerlahairoi; behold, it is between Kadesh and Bered.

Summary

After Sarai asked Abraham to sleep with Hagar, she became pregnant. From then on, she began to despise her mistress, Sarai, who abused her until she ran away from home. Here, the angel of the Lord found Hagar in the wilderness by a fountain of water. During this encounter, the angel of the Lord:

- Confirmed Sarai's authority upon Hagar by calling her "Sarai's maid"

- Instructed her to return back under Sarai's authority

- Promised to multiply her seed exceedingly and prophesied about her pregnancy and the baby that should come out

This encounter re-established order and authority for Hagar and Sarai, and the prophecies brought joy and happiness to Hagar.

4. **Genesis 18:1-22**

1 And the Lord appeared unto him in the plains of Mamre: and he sat in the tent door in the heat of the day;

2 And he lift up his eyes and looked, and, lo, three men stood by him: and when he saw them, he ran to meet them from the tent door, and bowed himself toward the ground,

3 And said, My Lord, if now I have found favour in thy sight, pass not away, I pray thee, from thy servant:

4 Let a little water, I pray you, be fetched, and wash your feet, and rest yourselves under the tree:

5 And I will fetch a morsel of bread, and comfort ye your hearts; after that ye shall pass on: for therefore are ye come to your servant. And they said, So do, as thou hast said.

6 And Abraham hastened into the tent unto Sarah, and said, Make ready quickly three measures of fine meal, knead it, and make cakes upon the hearth.

7 And Abraham ran unto the herd, and fetcht a calf tender and good, and gave it unto a young man; and he hasted to dress it.

8 And he took butter, and milk, and the calf which he had dressed, and set it before them; and he stood by them under the tree, and they did eat.

9 And they said unto him, Where is Sarah thy wife? And he said, Behold, in the tent.

10 And he said, I will certainly return unto thee according to the time of life; and, lo, Sarah thy wife shall have a son. And Sarah heard it in the tent door, which was behind him.

11 Now Abraham and Sarah were old and well stricken in age; and it ceased to be with Sarah after the manner of women.

12 Therefore Sarah laughed within herself, saying, After I am waxed old shall I have pleasure, my lord being old also?

13 And the Lord said unto Abraham, Wherefore did Sarah laugh, saying, Shall I of a surety bear a child, which am old?

14 Is any thing too hard for the Lord? At the time appointed I will return unto thee, according to the time of life, and Sarah shall have a son.

15 Then Sarah denied, saying, I laughed not; for she was afraid. And he said, Nay; but thou didst laugh.

16 And the men rose up from thence, and looked toward Sodom: and Abraham went with them to bring them on the way.

17 And the Lord said, Shall I hide from Abraham that thing which I do;

18 Seeing that Abraham shall surely become a great and mighty nation, and all the nations of the earth shall be blessed in him?

19 For I know him, that he will command his children and his household after him, and they shall keep the way of the Lord, to do justice and judgment; that the Lord may bring upon Abraham that which he hath spoken of him.

20 And the Lord said, Because the cry of Sodom and Gomorrah is great, and because their sin is very grievous;

21 I will go down now, and see whether they have done altogether according to the cry of it, which is come unto me; and if not, I will know.

22 And the men turned their faces from thence, and went toward Sodom: but Abraham stood yet before the Lord.

Summary

God visited Abraham with two angels and took the appearance of three men, representing the trinity: Father, Son, and Holy Ghost. It seems that God pours Himself out into those two angels and they become three synchronized men. They open their mouths, speak, and close their mouths at the same time. Besides that, they act like any ordinary man. They had been sitting with Abraham eating natural food and drinking like any ordinary man. After eating, they prophesied to Sarah that she would become pregnant and give birth to a boy despite her advanced age. God announced to Abraham the destruction of Sodom and Gomorrah.

The angels kept their human appearance while God, at a certain point, seemed to have changed his and spoke to Abraham as the Lord. The two angels left, heading toward Sodom and Gomorrah, while the Lord remained and discussed his plans for the two cities with Abraham.

5. **Genesis 19:1-26**

1 And there came two angels to Sodom at even; and Lot sat in the gate of Sodom: and Lot seeing them rose up to meet them; and he bowed himself with his face toward the ground;

2 And he said, Behold now, my lords, turn in, I pray you, into your servant's house, and tarry all night, and wash your feet, and ye shall rise up early, and go on your ways. And they said, Nay; but we will abide in the street all night.

3 And he pressed upon them greatly; and they turned in unto him, and entered into his house; and he made them a feast, and did bake unleavened bread, and they did eat.

4 But before they lay down, the men of the city, even the men of Sodom, compassed the house round, both old and young, all the people from every quarter:

5 And they called unto Lot, and said unto him, Where are the men which came in to thee this night? bring them out unto us, that we may know them.

6 And Lot went out at the door unto them, and shut the door after him,

7 And said, I pray you, brethren, do not so wickedly.

8 Behold now, I have two daughters which have not known man; let me, I pray you, bring them out unto you, and do ye to them as is good in your eyes: only unto these men do nothing; for therefore came they under the shadow of my roof.

9 And they said, Stand back. And they said again, This one fellow came in to sojourn, and he will needs be a judge: now will we deal worse with thee, than with them. And they pressed sore upon the man, even Lot, and came near to break the door.

10 But the men put forth their hand, and pulled Lot into the house to them, and shut to the door.

11 And they smote the men that were at the door of the house with blindness, both small and great: so that they wearied themselves to find the door.

12 And the men said unto Lot, Hast thou here any besides? son in law, and thy sons, and thy

daughters, and whatsoever thou hast in the city, bring them out of this place:

13 For we will destroy this place, because the cry of them is waxen great before the face of the Lord; and the Lord hath sent us to destroy it.

14 And Lot went out, and spake unto his sons in law, which married his daughters, and said, Up, get you out of this place; for the Lord will destroy this city. But he seemed as one that mocked unto his sons in law.

15 And when the morning arose, then the angels hastened Lot, saying, Arise, take thy wife, and thy two daughters, which are here; lest thou be consumed in the iniquity of the city.

16 And while he lingered, the men laid hold upon his hand, and upon the hand of his wife, and upon the hand of his two daughters; the Lord being merciful unto him: and they brought him forth, and set him without the city.

17 And it came to pass, when they had brought them forth abroad, that he said, Escape for thy life; look not behind thee, neither stay thou in all the plain; escape to the mountain, lest thou be consumed.

18 And Lot said unto them, Oh, not so, my Lord:

19 Behold now, thy servant hath found grace in thy sight, and thou hast magnified thy mercy, which thou hast shewed unto me in saving my life; and I

cannot escape to the mountain, lest some evil take me, and I die:

20 Behold now, this city is near to flee unto, and it is a little one: Oh, let me escape thither, (is it not a little one?) and my soul shall live.

21 And he said unto him, See, I have accepted thee concerning this thing also, that I will not overthrow this city, for the which thou hast spoken.

22 Haste thee, escape thither; for I cannot do anything till thou become thither. Therefore the name of the city was called Zoar.

23 The sun was risen upon the earth when Lot entered into Zoar.

24 Then the Lord rained upon Sodom and upon Gomorrah brimstone and fire from the Lord out of heaven;

25 And he overthrew those cities, and all the plain, and all the inhabitants of the cities, and that which grew upon the ground.

26 But his wife looked back from behind him, and she became a pillar of salt.

Summary

Having left Abraham's house, the two angels arrive in Sodom. Lot welcomes them at the entrance to the city and insists that they spend the night at his house.

They eventually accept Lot's invitation, enter his house, and partake of the feast he has prepared for them.

All the men in the city, from the youngest to the oldest, surround Lot's house and demand that he bring them out so that they can sexually abuse them. Lot refuses and instead offers them his two virgin daughters.

They lose their temper and threaten to attack Lot and his family and attack the two angels. But the angels strike them blind, save Lot and his family, and urge them to leave the city, announcing to them that they will destroy it.

Faced with Lot's hesitation, the angels forcefully lead them out of the city, warning him, his wife, and his two daughters not to look back no matter what happens.

However, during their escape, Lot's wife disobeys, looks back, and turns into a pillar of salt.

God rains fire and brimstone on Sodom and Gomorrah, destroying them completely.

6. Genesis 21:15-19

15 And the water was spent in the bottle, and she cast the child under one of the shrubs.

16 And she went, and sat her down over against him a good way off, as it were a bow shot: for she said, Let me not see the death of the child. And she sat over against him, and lift up her voice, and wept.

17 And God heard the voice of the lad; and the angel of God called to Hagar out of heaven, and said unto her, What aileth thee, Hagar? fear not; for God hath heard the voice of the lad where he is.

18 Arise, lift up the lad, and hold him in thine hand; for I will make him a great nation.

19 And God opened her eyes, and she saw a well of water; and she went, and filled the bottle with water, and gave the lad drink.

Summary

Hagar and her son Ishmael had been sent away by Abraham at Sarah's request. Having lost their way in the desert, they exhausted their supply of water. Not wanting to helplessly witness the death of her child, Hagar leaves Ishmaël crying under a bush and goes to stand opposite him at a good distance.

God, hearing the child's cry, sent an angel to their aid. This angel reassures Hagar, communicates to her the prophecies relating to the child—namely that he will become a great nation—and opens her eyes to see the well of water, which was nearby.

7. **Genesis 22:11-15**

    11 And the angel of the Lord called unto him out of heaven, and said, Abraham, Abraham: and he said, Here am I.

    12 And he said, Lay not thine hand upon the lad, neither do thou anything unto him: for now I know

that thou fearest God, seeing thou hast not withheld thy son, thine only son from me.

13 And Abraham lifted up his eyes, and looked, and behold behind him a ram caught in a thicket by his horns: and Abraham went and took the ram, and offered him up for a burnt offering in the stead of his son.

14 And Abraham called the name of that place Jehovah Jireh: as it is said to this day, In the mount of the Lord it shall be seen.

15 And the angel of the Lord called unto Abraham out of heaven the second time,

16 And said, By myself have I sworn, saith the Lord, for because thou hast done this thing, and hast not withheld thy son, thine only son:

17 That in blessing I will bless thee, and in multiplying I will multiply thy seed as the stars of the heaven, and as the sand which is upon the sea shore; and thy seed shall possess the gate of his enemies;

18 And in thy seed shall all the nations of the earth be blessed; because thou hast obeyed my voice.

Summary

As Abraham prepares to sacrifice his son Isaac in response to God's request, the angel of the Lord eagerly intervenes and prevents him. He asks Abraham not to harm Isaac and informs him that God now knows that he fears Him because he was willing to offer his only son as a sacrifice in obedience God's instruction.

Abraham then looks up and sees a ram trapped in a thicket by its horns. He takes it and offers it as a burnt offering in place of his son.

Abraham gives this place the name Jehovah Jireh, which means "The Lord will provide."

The angel renews God's blessings on Abraham, promising to multiply his descendants like the stars in the sky and the sand on the seashore.

8. Genesis 24:7-40

7 The Lord God of heaven, which took me from my father's house, and from the land of my kindred, and which spake unto me, and that sware unto me, saying, Unto thy seed will I give this land; he shall send his angel before thee, and thou shalt take a wife unto my son from thence.

8 And if the woman will not be willing to follow thee, then thou shalt be clear from this my oath: only bring not my son thither again.

9 And the servant put his hand under the thigh of Abraham his master, and sware to him concerning that matter.

10 And the servant took ten camels of the camels of his master, and departed; for all the goods of his master were in his hand: and he arose, and went to Mesopotamia, unto the city of Nahor.

11 And he made his camels to kneel down without the city by a well of water at the time of the evening, even the time that women go out to draw water.

12 And he said O Lord God of my master Abraham, I pray thee, send me good speed this day, and shew kindness unto my master Abraham.

13 Behold, I stand here by the well of water; and the daughters of the men of the city come out to draw water:

14 And let it come to pass, that the damsel to whom I shall say, Let down thy pitcher, I pray thee, that I may drink; and she shall say, Drink, and I will give thy camels drink also: let the same be she that thou hast appointed for thy servant Isaac; and thereby shall I know that thou hast shewed kindness unto my master.

15 And it came to pass, before he had done speaking, that, behold, Rebekah came out, who was born to Bethuel, son of Milcah, the wife of Nahor, Abraham's brother, with her pitcher upon her shoulder.

16 And the damsel was very fair to look upon, a virgin, neither had any man known her: and she went down to the well, and filled her pitcher, and came up.

17 And the servant ran to meet her, and said, Let me, I pray thee, drink a little water of thy pitcher.

18 And she said, Drink, my lord: and she hasted, and let down her pitcher upon her hand, and gave him drink.

19 And when she had done giving him drink, she said, I will draw water for thy camels also, until they have done drinking.

20 And she hasted, and emptied her pitcher into the trough, and ran again unto the well to draw water, and drew for all his camels.

21 And the man wondering at her held his peace, to wit whether the Lord had made his journey prosperous or not.

22 And it came to pass, as the camels had done drinking, that the man took a golden earring of half a shekel weight, and two bracelets for her hands of ten shekels weight of gold;

23 And said, Whose daughter art thou? tell me, I pray thee: is there room in thy father's house for us to lodge in?

24 And she said unto him, I am the daughter of Bethuel the son of Milcah, which she bare unto Nahor.

25 She said moreover unto him, We have both straw and provender enough, and room to lodge in.

26 And the man bowed down his head, and worshipped the Lord.

27 And he said, Blessed be the Lord God of my master Abraham, who hath not left destitute my

master of his mercy and his truth: I being in the way, the Lord led me to the house of my master's brethren.

28 And the damsel ran, and told them of her mother's house these things.

29 And Rebekah had a brother, and his name was Laban: and Laban ran out unto the man, unto the well.

30 And it came to pass, when he saw the earring and bracelets upon his sister's hands, and when he heard the words of Rebekah his sister, saying, Thus spake the man unto me; that he came unto the man; and, behold, he stood by the camels at the well.

31 And he said, Come in, thou blessed of the Lord; wherefore standest thou without? for I have prepared the house, and room for the camels.

32 And the man came into the house: and he ungirded his camels, and gave straw and provender for the camels, and water to wash his feet, and the men's feet that were with him.

33 And there was set meat before him to eat: but he said, I will not eat, until I have told mine errand. And he said, Speak on.

34 And he said, I am Abraham's servant.

35 And the Lord hath blessed my master greatly; and he is become great: and he hath given him flocks, and herds, and silver, and gold, and

menservants, and maidservants, and camels, and asses.

36 And Sarah my master's wife bare a son to my master when she was old: and unto him hath he given all that he hath.

37 And my master made me swear, saying, Thou shalt not take a wife to my son of the daughters of the Canaanites, in whose land I dwell:

38 But thou shalt go unto my father's house, and to my kindred, and take a wife unto my son.

39 And I said unto my master, Peradventure the woman will not follow me.

40 And he said unto me, The Lord, before whom I walk, will send his angel with thee, and prosper thy way; and thou shalt take a wife for my son of my kindred, and of my father's house:

Summary

Abraham makes his servant swear to go to his native country and precisely to his family in order to bring back a wife for his son Isaac, emphasizing that he must not marry a Canaanite woman. He informs the servant that the Lord will send his angel to accompany him on the journey and that he will be released from his oath if the woman refuses to come.

The servant leaves with camels and goods and travels to Nahor in Mesopotamia, where Abraham's family resides. Arriving at the city well, the servant asks God that the chosen woman be the one who gives him water when he asks and also waters his camels. Immediately, Rebekah arrives at the well and fulfills his request by giving him water and watering his camels.

The servant inquires about her family and discovers that she is the daughter of Bethuel, the nephew of Abraham.

Rebekah returns home and recounts her meeting with Abraham's servant. His brother Laban goes to the well and takes the servant home. The servant explains his mission and tells the story of his prayer at the well and the oath he had made to Abraham to bring back a bride from his family to Isaac.

Laban and Bethuel, Rebekah's father, recognize that it is the work of the Lord and give their blessing for Rebekah to go and marry Isaac. The servant gives gifts of gold and silver to Rebekah and her family as a token of his gratitude.

The servant's mission was successful, and he was protected on the way out and back by the angel of God, as Abraham had mentioned.

9. **Genesis 28:10-12**

10 And Jacob went out from Beersheba, and went toward Haran.

11 And he lighted upon a certain place, and tarried there all night, because the sun was set; and he took of the stones of that place, and put them for his pillows, and lay down in that place to sleep.

12 And he dreamed, and behold a ladder set up on the earth, and the top of it reached to heaven: and behold the angels of God ascending and descending on it.

Summary

Jacob, son of Isaac, travels from Beersheba to Haran. At a certain point, he decides to stop to spend the night because it was dark. During his sleep, he has a dream where he sees a ladder that connects heaven and earth, and the angels of God go up and down on this ladder. At the top of the ladder stood the Lord God himself speaking to him.

10. Genesis 31:11-13

11 And the angel of God spake unto me in a dream, saying, Jacob: And I said, Here am I.

12 And he said, Lift up now thine eyes, and see, all the rams which leap upon the cattle are ringstraked, speckled, and grisled: for I have seen all that Laban doeth unto thee.

13 I am the God of Bethel, where thou anointedst the pillar, and where thou vowedst a vow unto me: now arise, get thee out from this land, and return unto the land of thy kindred.

Summary

Jacob, who has worked for his uncle Laban for many years, is about to leave to return to his homeland with his family and his flocks.

He calls Rachel and Leah, his wives, to explain his dream where he saw spotted, speckled, and streaked goats mating with the flock. Jacob interprets this dream as a sign from God, indicating that it is time for him to return to his country. He knows that God is with him and has blessed him, even despite the deceptions of Laban, who unilaterally changed the terms of their agreement time and time again.

11. Genesis 32:1-2

1 And Jacob went on his way, and the angels of God met him.

2 And when Jacob saw them, he said, This is God's host: and he called the name of that place Mahanaim.

Summary

Jacob continues his journey until he arrives at a place where he meets a group of angels of God. By their presence, he recognizes that God is there and that this place is important. He named the place "The Camp of God" or "Mahanaim" in Hebrew. This naming highlights Jacob's awareness of the spiritual significance of the place and the divine protection he receives as he is about to meet his brother Esau, whom he has not seen since he stole the blessing Isaac meant for him.

12. Genesis 48:15-16

15 And he blessed Joseph, and said, God, before whom my fathers Abraham and Isaac did walk, the God which fed me all my life long unto this day,

16 The Angel which redeemed me from all evil, bless the lads; and let my name be named on them, and the name of my fathers Abraham and Isaac; and let them grow into a multitude in the midst of the earth.

Summary

In this text, Jacob expresses his deep emotions as he prepares to bless Ephraim and Manasseh, the sons of Joseph. He recognizes God's angels' intervention and direction throughout his life, from his ancestors Abraham and Isaac to his own experiences. He blessed Ephraim and Manasseh and prayed that God, who had been the shepherd and guide of his family, would bless these two boys to carry on the name and legacy of their ancestors, Abraham and Isaac, and that their descendants would become a great and numerous people.

Chapter 2
Angels in the Book of Exodus

1. **Exodus 3:1-2**

   1 Now Moses kept the flock of Jethro his father in law, the priest of Midian: and he led the flock to the backside of the desert, and came to the mountain of God, even to Horeb.

   2 And the angel of the LORD appeared unto him in a flame of fire out of the midst of a bush: and he looked, and, behold, the bush burned with fire, and the bush was not consumed.

   Summary

   After fleeing Egypt, Moses settled in the land of Midian, where he tended the flock of his father-in-law, Jethro. He leads the flock behind the desert and then goes to Horeb, the mountain of God, where the angel of the Lord appears to him in a burning bush but which is not consumed. This intriguing phenomenon attracts his attention, and he decides to get closer to it.

2. **Exodus 14:19**

   And the angel of God, which went before the camp of Israel, removed and went behind them; and the pillar of the cloud went from before their face, and stood behind them:

   Summary

   The angel of God, who led and guided the Israelites in the form of a pillar of cloud during the day, moves from in front of the Israelite camp to behind them. This movement of the angel creates a protective barrier that secures the Israelites' flight against the pursuit of the Egyptian army. Through this barrier, the angel brings darkness into the Egyptian camp, which cannot attack the children of Israel, while bringing light to the Israelites, who can continue to advance.

3. **Exodus 23:20-23**

   20 Behold, I send an Angel before thee, to keep thee in the way, and to bring thee into the place which I have prepared.

   21 Beware of him, and obey his voice, provoke him not; for he will not pardon your transgressions: for my name is in him.

   22 But if thou shalt indeed obey his voice, and do all that I speak; then I will be an enemy unto thine enemies, and an adversary unto thine adversaries.

   23 For mine Angel shall go before thee, and bring thee in unto the Amorites, and the Hittites, and the

Perizzites, and the Canaanites, the Hivites, and the Jebusites: and I will cut them off.

Summary

God informs the people of Israel that an angel will go before them to guard them and guide them on their journey to the land he promised to give them. However, He warns them to avoid any rebellion and disobedience because their success and their safety in this journey depends on their behavior toward this angel, and he will not forgive their transgressions.

God informs the Israelites that the angel bears His name, which reflects his connection with God himself, thereby identifying the source of his authority.

God assures the Israelites that if they obey the voice of the angel, he will be the enemy of their enemies and the adversary of their adversaries.

In summary, the protection of the children of Israel is conditional on their obedience to the voice of the angel.

4. Exodus 25:18-22

18 And thou shalt make two cherubims of gold, of beaten work shalt thou make them, in the two ends of the mercy seat.

19 And make one cherub on the one end, and the other cherub on the other end: even of the mercy

seat shall ye make the cherubims on the two ends thereof.

20 And the cherubims shall stretch forth their wings on high, covering the mercy seat with their wings, and their faces shall look one to another; toward the mercy seat shall the faces of the cherubims be.

21 And thou shalt put the mercy seat above upon the ark; and in the ark thou shalt put the testimony that I shall give thee.

22 And there I will meet with thee, and I will commune with thee from above the mercy seat, from between the two cherubims which are upon the ark of the testimony, of all things which I will give thee in commandment unto the children of Israel.

Summary

God instructs Moses to make a solid gold-covered mercy seat for the Ark of the Covenant, which will serve as a place of atonement. The mercy seat will consist of two cherubim made of beaten gold, placed at each end, facing each other, and covering the mercy seat with their wings. The cherubim, who are angelic beings, must be made one piece with the mercy seat.

God explains that it will be the meeting place between Him and Moses, a symbol of His presence and the communication between Him and the Israelites.

God further emphasizes its importance, stating that it will be located above the Ark of the Covenant and will contain the tablets inscribed with the Ten Commandments. God will speak with Moses from the top of the mercy seat, between the two cherubim.

5. **Exodus 26:1-31**

1 Moreover thou shalt make the tabernacle with ten curtains of fine twined linen, and blue, and purple, and scarlet: with cherubims of cunning work shalt thou make them.

2 The length of one curtain shall be eight and twenty cubits, and the breadth of one curtain four cubits: and every one of the curtains shall have one measure.

3 The five curtains shall be coupled together one to another; and other five curtains shall be coupled one to another.

4 And thou shalt make loops of blue upon the edge of the one curtain from the selvedge in the coupling; and likewise shalt thou make in the uttermost edge of another curtain, in the coupling of the second.

5 Fifty loops shalt thou make in the one curtain, and fifty loops shalt thou make in the edge of the curtain that is in the coupling of the second; that the loops may take hold one of another.

6 And thou shalt make fifty taches of gold, and couple the curtains together with the taches: and it shall be one tabernacle.

7 And thou shalt make curtains of goats' hair to be a covering upon the tabernacle: eleven curtains shalt thou make.

8 The length of one curtain shall be thirty cubits, and the breadth of one curtain four cubits: and the eleven curtains shall be all of one measure.

9 And thou shalt couple five curtains by themselves, and six curtains by themselves, and shalt double the sixth curtain in the forefront of the tabernacle.

10 And thou shalt make fifty loops on the edge of the one curtain that is outmost in the coupling, and fifty loops in the edge of the curtain which coupleth the second.

11 And thou shalt make fifty taches of brass, and put the taches into the loops, and couple the tent together, that it may be one.

12 And the remnant that remaineth of the curtains of the tent, the half curtain that remaineth, shall hang over the backside of the tabernacle.

13 And a cubit on the one side, and a cubit on the other side of that which remaineth in the length of the curtains of the tent, it shall hang over the sides of the tabernacle on this side and on that side, to cover it.

14 And thou shalt make a covering for the tent of rams' skins dyed red, and a covering above of badgers' skins.

15 And thou shalt make boards for the tabernacle of shittim wood standing up.

16 Ten cubits shall be the length of a board, and a cubit and a half shall be the breadth of one board.

17 Two tenons shall there be in one board, set in order one against another: thus shalt thou make for all the boards of the tabernacle.

18 And thou shalt make the boards for the tabernacle, twenty boards on the south side southward.

19 And thou shalt make forty sockets of silver under the twenty boards; two sockets under one board for his two tenons, and two sockets under another board for his two tenons.

20 And for the second side of the tabernacle on the north side there shall be twenty boards:

21 And their forty sockets of silver; two sockets under one board, and two sockets under another board.

22 And for the sides of the tabernacle westward thou shalt make six boards.

23 And two boards shalt thou make for the corners of the tabernacle in the two sides.

24 And they shall be coupled together beneath, and they shall be coupled together above the head of it unto one ring: thus shall it be for them both; they shall be for the two corners.

25 And they shall be eight boards, and their sockets of silver, sixteen sockets; two sockets under one board, and two sockets under another board.

26 And thou shalt make bars of shittim wood; five for the boards of the one side of the tabernacle,

27 And five bars for the boards of the other side of the tabernacle, and five bars for the boards of the side of the tabernacle, for the two sides westward.

28 And the middle bar in the midst of the boards shall reach from end to end.

29 And thou shalt overlay the boards with gold, and make their rings of gold for places for the bars: and thou shalt overlay the bars with gold.

30 And thou shalt rear up the tabernacle according to the fashion thereof which was shewed thee in the mount.

31 And thou shalt make a vail of blue, and purple, and scarlet, and fine twined linen of cunning work: with cherubims shall it be made:

Summary

This text describes the materials and dimensions of the curtains that would form the interior covering of the tabernacle. The curtains were to be made of fine linen and fabrics dyed in blues, purples, and scarlets with artistically crafted cherub motifs.

There are instructions for building the tent curtains and the outer covering of the tabernacle and for making the boards and bases that formed the frame of the tabernacle.

The blue, purple, and crimson veil that would serve to separate the holy place from the most holy place was to be made of fine twisted linen and artistically worked, with representations of cherubim.

6. Exodus 32:34

Therefore now go, lead the people unto the place of which I have spoken unto thee: behold, mine Angel shall go before thee: nevertheless in the day when I visit I will visit their sin upon them.

Summary

In this text, God confirms to Moses that the angel will continue his mission to accompany Israel to their destination despite their disobedience and rebellion. However, everyone will be held responsible for their actions. He will punish the people of Israel at the appropriate time.

7. Exodus 33:1-3

1 And the Lord said unto Moses, Depart, and go up hence, thou and the people which thou hast brought up out of the land of Egypt, unto the land which I sware unto Abraham, to Isaac, and to Jacob, saying, Unto thy seed will I give it:

2 And I will send an angel before thee; and I will drive out the Canaanite, the Amorite, and the Hittite, and the Perizzite, the Hivite, and the Jebusite:

3 Unto a land flowing with milk and honey: for I will not go up in the midst of thee; for thou art a stiffnecked people: lest I consume thee in the way.

Summary

God commands Moses to break camp and advance toward Canaan to confront the Canaanites, Amorites, Hittites, Perizzites, Hivites, and Jebusites. He informs him that, given the rebellious attitude of the people, He will not personally accompany them into battle. However, He will send an angel ahead of them to drive out the current inhabitants of the land.

8. Exodus 36:8-35

8 And every wise hearted man among them that wrought the work of the tabernacle made ten curtains of fine twined linen, and blue, and purple, and scarlet: with cherubims of cunning work made he them.

9 The length of one curtain was twenty and eight cubits, and the breadth of one curtain four cubits: the curtains were all of one size.

10 And he coupled the five curtains one unto another: and the other five curtains he coupled one unto another.

11 And he made loops of blue on the edge of one curtain from the selvedge in the coupling: likewise he made in the uttermost side of another curtain, in the coupling of the second.

12 Fifty loops made he in one curtain, and fifty loops made he in the edge of the curtain which was in the coupling of the second: the loops held one curtain to another.

13 And he made fifty taches of gold, and coupled the curtains one unto another with the taches: so it became one tabernacle.

14 And he made curtains of goats' hair for the tent over the tabernacle: eleven curtains he made them.

15 The length of one curtain was thirty cubits, and four cubits was the breadth of one curtain: the eleven curtains were of one size.

16 And he coupled five curtains by themselves, and six curtains by themselves.

17 And he made fifty loops upon the uttermost edge of the curtain in the coupling, and fifty loops made he upon the edge of the curtain which coupleth the second.

18 And he made fifty taches of brass to couple the tent together, that it might be one.

19 And he made a covering for the tent of rams' skins dyed red, and a covering of badgers' skins above that.

20 And he made boards for the tabernacle of shittim wood, standing up.

21 The length of a board was ten cubits, and the breadth of a board one cubit and a half.

22 One board had two tenons, equally distant one from another: thus did he make for all the boards of the tabernacle.

23 And he made boards for the tabernacle; twenty boards for the south side southward:

24 And forty sockets of silver he made under the twenty boards; two sockets under one board for his two tenons, and two sockets under another board for his two tenons.

25 And for the other side of the tabernacle, which is toward the north corner, he made twenty boards,

26 And their forty sockets of silver; two sockets under one board, and two sockets under another board.

27 And for the sides of the tabernacle westward he made six boards.

28 And two boards made he for the corners of the tabernacle in the two sides.

29 And they were coupled beneath, and coupled together at the head thereof, to one ring: thus he did to both of them in both the corners.

30 And there were eight boards; and their sockets were sixteen sockets of silver, under every board two sockets.

31 And he made bars of shittim wood; five for the boards of the one side of the tabernacle,

32 And five bars for the boards of the other side of the tabernacle, and five bars for the boards of the tabernacle for the sides westward.

33 And he made the middle bar to shoot through the boards from the one end to the other.

34 And he overlaid the boards with gold, and made their rings of gold to be places for the bars, and overlaid the bars with gold.

35 And he made a vail of blue, and purple, and scarlet, and fine twined linen: with cherubims made he it of cunning work.

Summary

These verses describe the construction of the curtains of the tabernacle that God had ordered with the representation of the cherubim, who are angelic beings. There, we also find the description of the construction of the curtains of the tent, the creation of the boards and supports for the framework of the Tabernacle, as well as the veil of the Most Holy Place, which, like the curtains of the Tabernacle, includes representations of cherubim. The text ends with the making of the screen for the entrance to the tabernacle.

9. Exodus 37:7-9

7 And he made two cherubims of gold, beaten out of one piece made he them, on the two ends of the mercy seat;

8 One cherub on the end on this side, and another cherub on the other end on that side: out of the mercy seat made he the cherubims on the two ends thereof.

9 And the cherubims spread out their wings on high, and covered with their wings over the mercy seat, with their faces one to another; even to the mercy seatward were the faces of the cherubims.

Summary

These verses describe the making and positioning, at the two ends of the mercy seat, of the two cherubim made of beaten gold as the Lord had ordered.

Chapter 3
Angels in the Book of Numbers

1. **Numbers 7:89**

   And when Moses was gone into the tabernacle of the congregation to speak with him, then he heard the voice of one speaking unto him from off the mercy seat that was upon the ark of testimony, from between the two cherubims: and he spake unto him.

   Summary

   This verse presents a meeting between God and Moses in the tabernacle, where the voice of God came out between the two cherubim from the top of the mercy seat, placed on the Ark of the Covenant. This confirms that God is among the children of Israel and that the tabernacle is his dwelling place.

2. **Numbers 20:16**

   And when we cried unto the LORD, he heard our voice, and sent an angel, and hath brought us forth out of Egypt: and, behold, we are in Kadesh, a city in the uttermost of thy border:

Summary

Moses sends messengers to the king of the Edomites, who are descendants of Esau, son of Isaac and twin brother of Jacob, asking permission to take the Israelites through their territory to go to Canaan. Moses informs him of the difficulties the Israelites faced and how, with the help of the angel of the Lord, they were able to leave Egypt and cross the desert. He promises to follow the path that will be indicated to them without deviating to go to the fields or consuming water from their wells. He guarantees that no damage will be caused to the land of Edom by their passage.

3. **Numbers 22:22-35**

22 And God's anger was kindled because he went: and the angel of the LORD stood in the way for an adversary against him. Now he was riding upon his ass, and his two servants were with him.

23 And the ass saw the angel of the LORD standing in the way, and his sword drawn in his hand: and the ass turned aside out of the way, and went into the field: and Balaam smote the ass, to turn her into the way.

24 But the angel of the LORD stood in a path of the vineyards, a wall being on this side, and a wall on that side.

25 And when the ass saw the angel of the LORD, she thrust herself unto the wall, and crushed

Balaam's foot against the wall: and he smote her again.

26 And the angel of the LORD went further, and stood in a narrow place, where was no way to turn either to the right hand or to the left.

27 And when the ass saw the angel of the LORD, she fell down under Balaam: and Balaam's anger was kindled, and he smote the ass with a staff.

28 And the Lord opened the mouth of the ass, and she said unto Balaam, What have I done unto thee, that thou hast smitten me these three times?

29 And Balaam said unto the ass, Because thou hast mocked me: I would there were a sword in mine hand, for now would I kill thee.

30 And the ass said unto Balaam, Am not I thine ass, upon which thou hast ridden ever since I was thine unto this day? was I ever wont to do so unto thee? and he said, Nay.

31 Then the LORD opened the eyes of Balaam, and he saw the angel of the LORD standing in the way, and his sword drawn in his hand: and he bowed down his head, and fell flat on his face.

32 And the angel of the LORD said unto him, Wherefore hast thou smitten thine ass these three times? behold, I went out to withstand thee, because thy way is perverse before me:

33 And the ass saw me, and turned from me these three times: unless she had turned from me, surely now also I had slain thee, and saved her alive.

34 And Balaam said unto the angel of the LORD, I have sinned; for I knew not that thou stoodest in the way against me: now therefore, if it displease thee, I will get me back again.

35 And the angel of the LORD said unto Balaam, Go with the men: but only the word that I shall speak unto thee, that thou shalt speak. So Balaam went with the princes of Balak.

Summary

Balaam ended up leaving with Balak's messengers to curse the children of Israel. However, God's anger is kindled against him since he does not respect His will. So God sends an angel to block his way. Balaam's donkey sees the angel, his drawn sword in his hand, blocking the path, but Balaam does not see him. Panicked, the donkey leaves the road and drags Balaam into a field, which angers him and pushes him to hit the animal to force it to move forward.

While trying to flee the angel, the donkey ends up crushing Balaam's foot. This reignites his anger and causes him to hit the donkey again.

The angel ends up trapping them in a narrow place with no way to turn away. In reaction, the donkey lies down under Balaam, who, out of anger, hits the donkey with his staff. The Lord opens the mouth of the donkey, who questions why Balaam is beating him. Balaam's eyes finally open, and he sees the angel standing before him with his sword drawn. The angel informs him that he has embarked on a path to perdition and explains that if the donkey had advanced, he would have killed it and spared the animal's life.

Balaam recognizes his sin and decides to return home, but the angel asks him to continue his journey to see Balak. However, he warns him that he should only speak the words that God puts in his mouth.

Chapter 4
Angels in the Book of Judges

1. **Judges 2:1-4**

   1 And an angel of the LORD came up from Gilgal to Bochim, and said, I made you to go up out of Egypt, and have brought you unto the land which I sware unto your fathers; and I said, I will never break my covenant with you.

   2 And ye shall make no league with the inhabitants of this land; ye shall throw down their altars: but ye have not obeyed my voice: why have ye done this?

   3 Wherefore I also said, I will not drive them out from before you; but they shall be as thorns in your sides, and their gods shall be a snare unto you.

   4 And it came to pass, when the angel of the LORD spake these words unto all the children of Israel, that the people lifted up their voice, and wept.

   Summary

   An angel of the Lord comes to the Israelites to deliver a message from God to the place called Bochim. The angel, after reminding them of God's covenant and how he brought them out of the land of Egypt to the Promised Land, reproaches them for their disobedience to his command to drive the Canaanite nations from the land and having alliances with them. He informs them that God will no longer drive out these nations before them and, therefore, they will become a stumbling block to them. Hearing this message, all the people began to cry and offer sacrifices to God, recognizing their sins.

2. Judges 5:23

Curse ye Meroz, said the angel of the LORD, curse ye bitterly the inhabitants thereof; because they came not to the help of the LORD, to the help of the LORD against the mighty.

Summary

This verse, taken from Deborah's song to celebrate the victory against Sisera, tells how the angel of the Lord cursed the territory of Meroz and its inhabitants because they did not take part in the battle against Sisera, leader of the army of Canaan, which oppressed Israel.

3. Judges 6:11-22

11 And there came an angel of the LORD, and sat under an oak which was in Ophrah, that pertained unto Joash the Abiezrite: and his son Gideon threshed wheat by the winepress, to hide it from the Midianites.

12 And the angel of the LORD appeared unto him, and said unto him, The LORD is with thee, thou mighty man of valour.

13 And Gideon said unto him, Oh my Lord, if the Lord be with us, why then is all this befallen us? and where be all his miracles which our fathers told us of, saying, Did not the Lord bring us up from Egypt? but now the Lord hath forsaken us, and delivered us into the hands of the Midianites.

14 And the Lord looked upon him, and said, Go in this thy might, and thou shalt save Israel from the hand of the Midianites: have not I sent thee?

15 And he said unto him, Oh my Lord, wherewith shall I save Israel? behold, my family is poor in Manasseh, and I am the least in my father's house.

16 And the Lord said unto him, Surely I will be with thee, and thou shalt smite the Midianites as one man.

17 And he said unto him, If now I have found grace in thy sight, then shew me a sign that thou talkest with me.

18 Depart not hence, I pray thee, until I come unto thee, and bring forth my present, and set it before thee. And he said, I will tarry until thou come again.

19 And Gideon went in, and made ready a kid, and unleavened cakes of an ephah of flour: the flesh he put in a basket, and he put the broth in a pot, and brought it out unto him under the oak, and presented it.

20 And the angel of God said unto him, Take the flesh and the unleavened cakes, and lay them upon this rock, and pour out the broth. And he did so.

21 Then the angel of the LORD put forth the end of the staff that was in his hand, and touched the flesh and the unleavened cakes; and there rose up fire out of the rock, and consumed the flesh and the unleavened cakes. Then the angel of the LORD departed out of his sight.

22 And when Gideon perceived that he was an angel of the LORD, Gideon said, Alas, O Lord GOD! for because I have seen an angel of the LORD face to face.

Summary

While the Israelites were living in caves and ravines because of the constant threat of the Midianites, an angel of the Lord appeared to Gideon, of the tribe of Manasseh, addressing him as a "mighty man of valor." For his part, Gideon only thinks about quickly harvesting the wheat and preparing it to be sheltered before the Midianites disembark because nothing will remain after their passage. This title, more than anything, surprises Gideon, who questions the angel's statement due to the dire circumstances the Israelites are facing. He asks why God allowed these things to happen to them and wonders where are the wonders that the ancestors told them. The angel of the Lord reassures him and affirms that he is the one who will save Israel from the Midianites and that God is with him. Reluctant and doubting his own abilities to accomplish such a task, Gideon asks for a sign to confirm that it is indeed God who is speaking to him, which was granted to him. Realizing that he has an encounter with the angel of the Lord and fearing for his life, Gideon believes that he is going to die. The angel reassures him and confirms that he will not die.

4. Judges 13:3-21

3 And the angel of the LORD appeared unto the woman, and said unto her, Behold now, thou art barren, and bearest not: but thou shalt conceive, and bear a son.

4 Now therefore beware, I pray thee, and drink not wine nor strong drink, and eat not any unclean thing:

5 For, lo, thou shalt conceive, and bear a son; and no razor shall come on his head: for the child shall be a Nazarite unto God from the womb: and he shall begin to deliver Israel out of the hand of the Philistines.

6 Then the woman came and told her husband, saying, A man of God came unto me, and his countenance was like the countenance of an angel of God, very terrible: but I asked him not whence he was, neither told he me his name:

7 But he said unto me, Behold, thou shalt conceive, and bear a son; and now drink no wine nor strong drink, neither eat any unclean thing: for the child

shall be a Nazarite to God from the womb to the day of his death.

8 Then Manoah intreated the Lord, and said, O my Lord, let the man of God which thou didst send come again unto us, and teach us what we shall do unto the child that shall be born.

9 And God hearkened to the voice of Manoah; and the angel of God came again unto the woman as she sat in the field: but Manoah her husband was not with her.

10 And the woman made haste, and ran, and shewed her husband, and said unto him, Behold, the man hath appeared unto me, that came unto me the other day.

11 And Manoah arose, and went after his wife, and came to the man, and said unto him, Art thou the man that spakest unto the woman? And he said, I am.

12 And Manoah said, Now let thy words come to pass. How shall we order the child, and how shall we do unto him?

13 And the angel of the LORD said unto Manoah, Of all that I said unto the woman let her beware.

14 She may not eat of any thing that cometh of the vine, neither let her drink wine or strong drink, nor eat any unclean thing: all that I commanded her let her observe.

15 And Manoah said unto the angel of the LORD, I pray thee, let us detain thee, until we shall have made ready a kid for thee.

16 And the angel of the LORD said unto Manoah, Though thou detain me, I will not eat of thy bread: and if thou wilt offer a burnt offering, thou must offer it unto the LORD. For Manoah knew not that he was an angel of the LORD.

17 And Manoah said unto the angel of the LORD, What is thy name, that when thy sayings come to pass we may do thee honour?

18 And the angel of the LORD said unto him, Why askest thou thus after my name, seeing it is secret?

19 So Manoah took a kid with a meat offering, and offered it upon a rock unto the LORD: and the angel did wondrously; and Manoah and his wife looked on.

20 For it came to pass, when the flame went up toward heaven from off the altar, that the angel of the LORD ascended in the flame of the altar. And Manoah and his wife looked on it, and fell on their faces to the ground.

21 But the angel of the LORD did no more appear to Manoah and to his wife. Then Manoah knew that he was an angel of the LORD.

Summary

While the people of Israel were undergoing a period of oppression at the hands of the Philistines, an angel of the Lord appears to Manoah's wife, who was barren, and tells her that she will become pregnant and give birth to a son. He orders her not to drink wine or strong drink nor to consume anything impure during her pregnancy. He also states that this child's head must never be shaved and he will be devoted to God all his life from his mother's womb. Manoah's wife communicates to him the angel's message and instructions. Manoah prays to God and asks for the angel to return and provide him with more explanations. God answers Manoah's prayer, and the angel appears again and speaks to them, both confirming the previous message and repeating the instructions. Manoah offers a sacrifice to God on a rock, and as the flames rise from the altar, the angel ascends to heaven in their midst.

Chapter 5
Angels in the books of Samuel

1. **1 Samuel 4:2-4**

   2 And the Philistines put themselves in array against Israel: and when they joined battle, Israel was smitten before the Philistines: and they slew of the army in the field about four thousand men.

   3 And when the people were come into the camp, the elders of Israel said, Wherefore hath the Lord smitten us to day before the Philistines? Let us fetch the ark of the covenant of the Lord out of Shiloh unto us, that, when it cometh among us, it may save us out of the hand of our enemies.

   4 So the people sent to Shiloh, that they might bring from thence the ark of the covenant of the LORD of hosts, which dwelleth between the cherubims: and the two sons of Eli, Hophni and Phinehas, were there with the ark of the covenant of God.

   Summary

   The Israelites were fighting against the Philistines. The children of Israel were beaten and lost four thousand men on the battlefield. The elders of

Israel gathered together and discussed why they had been defeated by the Philistines. They resolved to fetch the Ark of the Covenant of the Lord from Shiloh and bring it to the battlefield to guarantee them victory. They brought from Shiloh the Ark of the Covenant, where the Lord of hosts sits among the cherubim. The two sons of Eli the priest, Hophni and Phinehas, were also present with the Ark.

2. 1 Samuel 29:9

And Achish answered and said to David, I know that thou art good in my sight, as an angel of God: notwithstanding the princes of the Philistines have said, He shall not go up with us to the battle.

Summary

Here, we find Achish, son of Maoch, king of Gath, expressing his confidence in David, who is part of his personal guard and who has been living among the Philistines for some time. Achish tells David that he is satisfied with his loyalty and that he is as blameless as an angel of God. He confirms that David is a reliable and faithful ally in his service.

3. 2 Samuel 6:2

And David arose, and went with all the people that were with him from Baale of Judah, to bring up from thence the ark of God, whose name is called by the name of the LORD of hosts that dwelleth between the cherubims.

Summary

David, having become king of Israel, gathers all the elite of Israel to move the Ark of the Covenant of the Lord, before which is invoked the name of the Lord, who resides between the cherubim, from Baale-Judah toward his home. The Ark is sacred. It symbolizes the presence of God among the Israelites and contains the stone tablets on which the Ten Commandments are written.

4. 2 Samuel 14:17-20

17 Then thine handmaid said, The word of my lord the king shall now be comfortable: for as an angel of God, so is my lord the king to discern good and bad: therefore the LORD thy God will be with thee.

18 Then the king answered and said unto the woman, Hide not from me, I pray thee, the thing that I shall ask thee. And the woman said, Let my lord the king now speak.

19 And the king said, Is not the hand of Joab with thee in all this? And the woman answered and said, As thy soul liveth, my lord the king, none can turn to the right hand or to the left from ought that my lord the king hath spoken: for thy servant Joab, he bade me, and he put all these words in the mouth of thine handmaid:

20 To fetch about this form of speech hath thy servant Joab done this thing: and my lord is wise, according to the wisdom of an angel of God, to know all things that are in the earth.

Summary

Tekoa's wife delivers the message Joab had prepared to King David, claiming to have two sons who fought, resulting in the death of one of them. She mentions how her entire family is pressuring her to hand over her last son to them so they can make him pay for his crime. She requests the king's intervention to save her son's life. David, moved by the woman's plea, agrees to help her. But above all, he asks if Joab, his commander, was not behind all this. The woman confirms that Joab did, in fact, make up the whole story and adds that he did it to give things another twist. She recognizes that the king, being as wise as an angel of God, will eventually understand everything. This ploy by Joab was intended to gain clemency from David toward his own son Absalom, who had been banished for killing his half-brother Amnon.

5. 2 Samuel 19:27

And he hath slandered thy servant unto my lord the king; but my lord the king is as an angel of God: do therefore what is good in thine eyes.

Summary

This text describes David's conversation with Mephibosheth upon returning from his flight during Absalom's rebellion. He questions why he had not accompanied him in his escape. Mephibosheth, to defend himself, argues that his servant slandered him to the king. However, he expresses the conviction that the king, being just and good like an angel of God, will make the best decision in the circumstances.

6. **2 Samuel 22:11**

   And he rode upon a cherub, and did fly: and he was seen upon the wings of the wind.

   Summary

   David describes in this passage a divine intervention on his behalf, where God rode on a cherub and flew on the wings of the wind. These images highlight God's quick and powerful action to help David in his difficult times.

7. **2 Samuel 24:16-17**

   16 And when the angel stretched out his hand upon Jerusalem to destroy it, the LORD repented him of the evil, and said to the angel that destroyed the people, It is enough: stay now thine hand. And the angel of the LORD was by the threshingplace of Araunah the Jebusite.

   17 And David spake unto the LORD when he saw the angel that smote the people, and said, Lo, I have sinned, and I have done wickedly: but these sheep, what have they done? let thine hand, I pray thee, be against me, and against my father's house.

   Summary

   David recognized that he had sinned by taking a census of the people. Among the three choices God had given through Gad the prophet, David accepted three days of plague as punishment. Following this choice, God sent an angel to bring the plague to the territory of Israel. When the angel, who stood on the property of Aravna the Jebusite, stretched out his hand to strike the city of Jerusalem, the Lord, having pity on that city, ordered him to turn away his hand. At the sight of the angel, David prayed and asked God that the angel's target be him and his father's house and not the people since it was he who sinned.

Chapter 6
Angels in the books of Kings

1. **1 Kings 6:23-35**

    23 And within the oracle he made two cherubims of olive tree, each ten cubits high.

    24 And five cubits was the one wing of the cherub, and five cubits the other wing of the cherub: from the uttermost part of the one wing unto the uttermost part of the other were ten cubits.

    25 And the other cherub was ten cubits: both the cherubims were of one measure and one size.

    26 The height of the one cherub was ten cubits, and so was it of the other.

    27 And he set the cherubims within the inner house: and they stretched forth the wings of the cherubims, so that the wing of the one touched the one wall, and the wing of the other cherub touched the other wall; and their wings touched one another in the midst of the house.

    28 And he overlaid the cherubims with gold.

29 And he carved all the walls of the house round about with carved figures of cherubims and palm trees and open flowers, within and without.

30 And the floors of the house he overlaid with gold, within and without.

31 And for the entering of the oracle he made doors of olive tree: the lintel and side posts were a fifth part of the wall.

32 The two doors also were of olive tree; and he carved upon them carvings of cherubims and palm trees and open flowers, and overlaid them with gold, and spread gold upon the cherubims, and upon the palm trees.

33 So also made he for the door of the temple posts of olive tree, a fourth part of the wall.

34 And the two doors were of fir tree: the two leaves of the one door were folding, and the two leaves of the other door were folding.

35 And he carved thereon cherubims and palm trees and open flowers: and covered them with gold fitted upon the carved work.

Summary

This text describes the size and position of the elaborate carvings of cherubs that adorned Solomon's Temple from the Most Holy Place to the exterior of the temple. These intricate carvings were on the walls, floors, doors, and door frames and were all covered in gold.

2. 1 Kings 7:29-36

29 And on the borders that were between the ledges were lions, oxen, and cherubims: and upon the ledges there was a base above: and beneath the lions and oxen were certain additions made of thin work.

30 And every base had four brasen wheels, and plates of brass: and the four corners thereof had undersetters: under the laver were undersetters molten, at the side of every addition.

31 And the mouth of it within the chapiter and above was a cubit: but the mouth thereof was round after the work of the base, a cubit and an half: and also upon the mouth of it were gravings with their borders, foursquare, not round.

32 And under the borders were four wheels; and the axletrees of the wheels were joined to the base: and the height of a wheel was a cubit and half a cubit.

33 And the work of the wheels was like the work of a chariot wheel: their axletrees, and their naves, and their felloes, and their spokes, were all molten.

34 And there were four undersetters to the four corners of one base: and the undersetters were of the very base itself.

35 And in the top of the base was there a round compass of half a cubit high: and on the top of the base the ledges thereof and the borders thereof were of the same.

36 For on the plates of the ledges thereof, and on the borders thereof, he graved cherubims, lions, and palm trees, according to the proportion of every one, and additions round about.

Summary

This text describes the brass bases, ten in number, that were in the temple. Each was made up of panels and uprights, and on the panels, which were between the uprights, there were sculptures of lions, oxen, and cherubim, which are angelic beings with wings.

3. 1 Kings 8:6-7

6 And the priests brought in the ark of the covenant of the LORD unto his place, into the oracle of the house, to the most holy place, even under the wings of the cherubims.

8:7 For the cherubims spread forth their two wings over the place of the ark, and the cherubims covered the ark and the staves thereof above.

Summary

The atmosphere that reigned when the priests carried the Ark of the Covenant during the inauguration of the temple was a deep feeling of awe and reverence. The text also recalls the contents of the Ark of the Covenant, in this case, the stone tablets on which the Ten Commandments were written, which symbolized the presence of God among the children of Israel. It also recalls the position of the Ark, which was placed under the cherubim, whose wings extended over the Ark, completely covering it.

4. 1 Kings 13:18

He said unto him, I am a prophet also as thou art; and an angel spake unto me by the word of the LORD, saying, Bring him back with thee into thine house, that he may eat bread and drink water. But he lied unto him.

Summary

The old prophet who lived in Bethel tricked the young prophet who was sent by God by lying to him, claiming that an angel of God had spoken to him and communicated a message contrary to that which had initially been communicated to the young prophet at knowing that he should neither eat bread nor drink water in this city. He will die because of his disobedience.

5. 1 Kings 19:5-7

5 And as he lay and slept under a juniper tree, behold, then an angel touched him, and said unto him, Arise and eat.

6 And he looked, and, behold, there was a cake baken on the coals, and a cruse of water at his head. And he did eat and drink, and laid him down again.

7 And the angel of the LORD came again the second time, and touched him, and said, Arise and eat; because the journey is too great for thee.

All Angels in the Bible

Summary

To escape Queen Jezebel's threat of death after his confrontation with the prophets of Baal, Elijah fled into the desert. Exhausted and discouraged, Elijah prays to God to take his life and then falls asleep under a broom tree. He is awakened twice by an angel who has prepared food for him and orders him to eat. After eating and drinking, the second meal gives him the strength to walk forty days and forty nights to reach the top of the mountain of God in Horeb.

6. 2 Kings 1:3-15

3 But the angel of the LORD said to Elijah the Tishbite, Arise, go up to meet the messengers of the king of Samaria, and say unto them, Is it not because there is not a God in Israel, that ye go to enquire of Baalzebub the god of Ekron?

4 Now therefore thus saith the Lord, Thou shalt not come down from that bed on which thou art gone up, but shalt surely die. And Elijah departed.

5 And when the messengers turned back unto him, he said unto them, Why are ye now turned back?

6 And they said unto him, There came a man up to meet us, and said unto us, Go, turn again unto the king that sent you, and say unto him, Thus saith the Lord, Is it not because there is not a God in Israel, that thou sendest to enquire of Baalzebub the god of Ekron? therefore thou shalt not come down from

that bed on which thou art gone up, but shalt surely die.

7 And he said unto them, What manner of man was he which came up to meet you, and told you these words?

8 And they answered him, He was an hairy man, and girt with a girdle of leather about his loins. And he said, It is Elijah the Tishbite.

9 Then the king sent unto him a captain of fifty with his fifty. And he went up to him: and, behold, he sat on the top of an hill. And he spake unto him, Thou man of God, the king hath said, Come down.

10 And Elijah answered and said to the captain of fifty, If I be a man of God, then let fire come down from heaven, and consume thee and thy fifty. And there came down fire from heaven, and consumed him and his fifty.

11 Again also he sent unto him another captain of fifty with his fifty. And he answered and said unto him, O man of God, thus hath the king said, Come down quickly.

12 And Elijah answered and said unto them, If I be a man of God, let fire come down from heaven, and consume thee and thy fifty. And the fire of God came down from heaven, and consumed him and his fifty.

13 And he sent again a captain of the third fifty with his fifty. And the third captain of fifty went up, and came and fell on his knees before Elijah, and

besought him, and said unto him, O man of God, I pray thee, let my life, and the life of these fifty thy servants, be precious in thy sight.

14 Behold, there came fire down from heaven, and burnt up the two captains of the former fifties with their fifties: therefore let my life now be precious in thy sight.

15 And the angel of the LORD said unto Elijah, Go down with him: be not afraid of him. And he arose, and went down with him unto the king.

Summary

Following a fall through the latticework of his upper room in Samaria, King Ahaziah is seriously injured and fears for his life. He sends messengers to Baal-Zebub, the god of Ekron, to determine whether he will recover from his wounds. While they are on their way, the angel of the Lord orders the prophet Elijah to intercept the messengers and then send them back to King Ahaziah with a message from God asking him why he sought advice from Baal-Zebub, a false god, instead of the God of Israel. Because of this, he will not recover and will die on his bed. Hearing this message, King Ahaziah, furious, sent to capture the prophet Elijah. Twice, the troops failed because Elijah commanded, each time, that fire would come down from heaven and consume them.

The captain of the third troop humbly implores Elijah's mercy for his life and that of his men. God asks Elijah to accompany this captain, and, going to the king, he transmits God's message to him in person.

7. **2 Kings 6:15-17**

    15 And when the servant of the man of God was risen early, and gone forth, behold, an host compassed the city both with horses and chariots. And his servant said unto him, Alas, my master! how shall we do?

    16 And he answered, Fear not: for they that be with us are more than they that be with them.

    17 And Elisha prayed, and said, Lord, I pray thee, open his eyes, that he may see. And the Lord opened the eyes of the young man; and he saw: and, behold, the mountain was full of horses and chariots of fire round about Elisha.

    Summary

    Elisha's servant wakes up one morning and finds the city surrounded by the Syrian army. Panicked, the servant runs to inform the prophet Elisha, who, while remaining calm and without fear, prays to the Lord to open his servant's eyes so that he can see. In response to Elisha's prayer, the servant's eyes open and he suddenly perceives the mountain around them is filled with horses and chariots of fire, representing a mighty angelic army surrounding the prophet Elisha.

8. 2 Kings 19:15-19

15 And Hezekiah prayed before the LORD, and said, O LORD God of Israel, which dwellest between the cherubims, thou art the God, even thou alone, of all the kingdoms of the earth; thou hast made heaven and earth.

16 Lord, bow down thine ear, and hear: open, Lord, thine eyes, and see: and hear the words of Sennacherib, which hath sent him to reproach the living God.

17 Of a truth, Lord, the kings of Assyria have destroyed the nations and their lands,

18 And have cast their gods into the fire: for they were no gods, but the work of men's hands, wood and stone: therefore they have destroyed them.

19 Now therefore, O Lord our God, I beseech thee, save thou us out of his hand, that all the kingdoms of the earth may know that thou art the Lord God, even thou only.

Summary

Sennacherib, the king of Assyria, sent Rabshakeh from Lachish to Jerusalem with a powerful army to besiege the city of Jerusalem. He sent Hezekiah a letter full of threats and insults against him and against the God of Israel. Upon receiving this letter, Hezekiah went to the house of the Lord, the temple in Jerusalem, and spread the letter before the Lord and prayed, saying, O LORD God of Israel, sit on the cherubim! Eternal! Incline thine ear, and hear.

Eternal! Open your eyes, and look. Hear the words of Sennacherib, who sent Rabshakeh to insult the living God. It is true, O LORD! that the kings of Assyria have destroyed the nations and ravaged their lands, and have cast their gods into the fire; but they were not gods, they were the works of human hands, wood and stone; and they destroyed them. Now, O LORD our God! Deliver us from the hand of Sennacherib, and let all the kingdoms of the earth know that you alone are God, O LORD.

9. 2 Kings 19:32-36

32 Therefore thus saith the Lord concerning the king of Assyria, He shall not come into this city, nor shoot an arrow there, nor come before it with shield, nor cast a bank against it.

33 By the way that he came, by the same shall he return, and shall not come into this city, saith the Lord.

34 For I will defend this city, to save it, for mine own sake, and for my servant David's sake.

35 And it came to pass that night, that the angel of the Lord went out, and smote in the camp of the Assyrians an hundred fourscore and five thousand: and when they arose early in the morning, behold, they were all dead corpses.

36 So Sennacherib king of Assyria departed, and went and returned, and dwelt at Nineveh.

All Angels in the Bible

Summary

God answers Hezekiah's prayer, through the prophet Isaiah, by reassuring him that the Assyrian king will not enter Jerusalem or shoot an arrow there. God promises to defend the city for himself and because of the promise He made to David. That same night, while the Assyrian army was camped around Jerusalem, the Lord sent an angel, who killed 185,000 Assyrian soldiers. When the inhabitants of Jerusalem woke up the next day, they found the Assyrian camp filled with corpses. Sennacherib, king of Assyria, retires in disgrace and returns to Nineveh.

Chapter 7
Angels in the books of Chronicles

1. 1 Chronicles 13:6

And David went up, and all Israel, to Baalah, that is, to Kirjathjearim, which belonged to Judah, to bring up thence the ark of God the LORD, that dwelleth between the cherubims, whose name is called on it.

Summary

In this text, King David summons all the leaders of Israel to Jerusalem, where he expresses his desire to bring back the Ark of the Covenant, which symbolizes the presence of God, from Kiriath-jearim, of the house of Abinadab. Following the agreement of the people, David went up to Baala in Kiriath-jearim, where the Ark of God was located, before which is called the name of the Lord who resides between the cherubim.

2. 1 Chronicles 21:12-30

12 Either three years' famine; or three months to be destroyed before thy foes, while that the sword of thine enemies overtaketh thee; or else three days the sword of the LORD, even the pestilence, in the

land, and the angel of the LORD destroying throughout all the coasts of Israel. Now therefore advise thyself what word I shall bring again to him that sent me.

13 And David said unto Gad, I am in a great strait: let me fall now into the hand of the Lord; for very great are his mercies: but let me not fall into the hand of man.

14 So the Lord sent pestilence upon Israel: and there fell of Israel seventy thousand men.

15 And God sent an angel unto Jerusalem to destroy it: and as he was destroying, the LORD beheld, and he repented him of the evil, and said to the angel that destroyed, It is enough, stay now thine hand. And the angel of the LORD stood by the threshingfloor of Ornan the Jebusite.

16 And David lifted up his eyes, and saw the angel of the LORD stand between the earth and the heaven, having a drawn sword in his hand stretched out over Jerusalem. Then David and the elders of Israel, who were clothed in sackcloth, fell upon their faces.

17 And David said unto God, Is it not I that commanded the people to be numbered? even I it is that have sinned and done evil indeed; but as for these sheep, what have they done? let thine hand, I pray thee, O Lord my God, be on me, and on my father's house; but not on thy people, that they should be plagued.

18 Then the angel of the LORD commanded Gad to say to David, that David should go up, and set up an altar unto the LORD in the threshingfloor of Ornan the Jebusite.

19 And David went up at the saying of Gad, which he spake in the name of the Lord.

20 And Ornan turned back, and saw the angel; and his four sons with him hid themselves. Now Ornan was threshing wheat.

21 And as David came to Ornan, Ornan looked and saw David, and went out of the threshingfloor, and bowed himself to David with his face to the ground.

22 Then David said to Ornan, Grant me the place of this threshingfloor, that I may build an altar therein unto the Lord: thou shalt grant it me for the full price: that the plague may be stayed from the people.

23 And Ornan said unto David, Take it to thee, and let my lord the king do that which is good in his eyes: lo, I give thee the oxen also for burnt offerings, and the threshing instruments for wood, and the wheat for the meat offering; I give it all.

24 And king David said to Ornan, Nay; but I will verily buy it for the full price: for I will not take that which is thine for the Lord, nor offer burnt offerings without cost.

25 So David gave to Ornan for the place six hundred shekels of gold by weight.

26 And David built there an altar unto the Lord, and offered burnt offerings and peace offerings, and called upon the Lord; and he answered him from heaven by fire upon the altar of burnt offering.

27 And the Lord commanded the angel; and he put up his sword again into the sheath thereof.

28 At that time when David saw that the Lord had answered him in the threshingfloor of Ornan the Jebusite, then he sacrificed there.

29 For the tabernacle of the Lord, which Moses made in the wilderness, and the altar of the burnt offering, were at that season in the high place at Gibeon.

30 But David could not go before it to enquire of God: for he was afraid because of the sword of the angel of the Lord.

Summary

In these verses, God was angry with David for having ordered, on his own, a census of the people of Israel. To punish him, He sent him the prophet Gad with these three choices of punishment: seven years of famine, three months of flight from his enemies, or three days during which the sword of the Lord and the pestilence will be in the land and the angel of the Lord will bring destruction throughout all the territory of Israel. Recognizing the seriousness of his act, David chose to fall into the hands of the Lord and opted for the three days of plague. The Lord sends an angel to stand near the threshing floor of Ornan the Jebusite and strike the land with a plague. 70,000 men were carried away by the scourge. As the angel struck the city of Jerusalem, God took pity on the people and commanded the angel to remove his hand from the city. At that moment, David's eyes were opened and he could see the angel standing between heaven and earth near the threshing floor of Ornan the Jebusite and having in his hand his drawn sword turned against Jerusalem. David prayed with the elders and asked God that his hand would be on him and on his father's house and that it would not cause a plague among the people of God. Through Gad the prophet, the angel of the Lord asks David to raise an altar to the Lord on the threshing floor of Ornan, the Jebusite. David goes to meet Ornan and offers to buy his threshing floor to build an altar for sacrifices to stop the plague. Ornan offers to give it to him free of charge, as well as the oxen and the wood for the offerings. However, David insists on paying, emphasizing that he will not offer sacrifices to God that cost him nothing. David builds the altar, offers sacrifices, and calls on the Lord. In response to his prayers and sacrifices, the Lord orders the angel to put away his sword, thus ending the plague.

3. **1 Chronicles 28:18**

And for the altar of incense refined gold by weight; and gold for the pattern of the chariot of the cherubims, that spread out their wings, and covered the ark of the covenant of the LORD.

All Angels in the Bible

Summary

David expressed a desire to build a house for the Ark of the Covenant, but God had chosen his son Solomon to accomplish this task in his place. Then David gathers and informs all of Israel's leaders—including tribal leaders, military commanders, and other leaders—of the plan and God's decision. He set about preparing the materials and resources needed for construction and provided detailed instructions to Solomon, describing the plans for the construction of the temple, its various rooms, and specifications regarding the furniture and utensils to be used in the service of the temple, and the golden cherubim, which spread their wings and cover the ark of the covenant of the Lord.

4. 2 Chronicles 3:7-14

7 He overlaid also the house, the beams, the posts, and the walls thereof, and the doors thereof, with gold; and graved cherubims on the walls.

8 And he made the most holy house, the length whereof was according to the breadth of the house, twenty cubits, and the breadth thereof twenty cubits: and he overlaid it with fine gold, amounting to six hundred talents.

9 And the weight of the nails was fifty shekels of gold. And he overlaid the upper chambers with gold.

10 And in the most holy house he made two cherubims of image work, and overlaid them with gold.

11 And the wings of the cherubims were twenty cubits long: one wing of the one cherub was five cubits, reaching to the wall of the house: and the other wing was likewise five cubits, reaching to the wing of the other cherub.

12 And one wing of the other cherub was five cubits, reaching to the wall of the house: and the other wing was five cubits also, joining to the wing of the other cherub.

13 The wings of these cherubims spread themselves forth twenty cubits: and they stood on their feet, and their faces were inward.

14 And he made the vail of blue, and purple, and crimson, and fine linen, and wrought cherubims thereon.

Summary

The passage describes the construction of Solomon's Temple, also known as the First Temple, in Jerusalem. It presents in detail the decorations and furniture of the most sacred part of the temple—namely the inner sanctuary or the Holy of Holies, the walls, the beams, the floors, and even the nails, the two large cherubim whose wings are deployed such that their combined span covered the entire width of the inner sanctuary, the veil, the pillars and entrance, and the bronze altar for sacrifices.

These verses provide a detailed description of the opulence and craftsmanship that went into building Solomon's Temple while emphasizing its importance as a central place of worship where God's presence resided.

5. 2 Chronicles 5:7-8

7 And the priests brought in the ark of the covenant of the LORD unto his place, to the oracle of the house, into the most holy place, even under the wings of the cherubims:

8 For the cherubims spread forth their wings over the place of the ark, and the cherubims covered the ark and the staves thereof above.

Summary

After Solomon built the temple, the priests brought the Ark of the Covenant into the Temple and placed it in the Most Holy Place under the wings of the cherubim.

6. 2 Chronicles 32:21

And the LORD sent an angel, which cut off all the mighty men of valour, and the leaders and captains in the camp of the king of Assyria. So he returned with shame of face to his own land. And when he was come into the house of his god, they that came forth of his own bowels slew him there with the sword.

J. Pitterson

Summary

In this verse, the context is the story of Hezekiah, king of Judah, who faces a military threat from Sennacherib, king of Assyria. Hezekiah had turned to the Lord for help and received a message from the prophet Isaiah, assuring him of God's intervention.

The angel of the Lord comes out in the middle of the night and strikes 185,000 soldiers of the Assyrian army. When the people of Jerusalem woke up the next morning, they found the Assyrian camp filled with corpses. Sennacherib, the Assyrian king, retired in disgrace to his country, where his sons killed him by the sword in the temple of his god.

Chapter 8
Angels in the Book of Job

1. **Job 1:6-12**

   6 Now there was a day when the sons of God came to present themselves before the Lord, and Satan came also among them.

   7 And the Lord said unto Satan, Whence comest thou? Then Satan answered the Lord, and said, From going to and fro in the earth, and from walking up and down in it.

   8 And the Lord said unto Satan, Hast thou considered my servant Job, that there is none like him in the earth, a perfect and an upright man, one that feareth God, and escheweth evil?

   9 Then Satan answered the Lord, and said, Doth Job fear God for nought?

   10 Hast not thou made an hedge about him, and about his house, and about all that he hath on every side? thou hast blessed the work of his hands, and his substance is increased in the land.

   11 But put forth thine hand now, and touch all that he hath, and he will curse thee to thy face.

12 And the Lord said unto Satan, Behold, all that he hath is in thy power; only upon himself put not forth thine hand. So Satan went forth from the presence of the Lord.

Summary

This passage describes a scene that takes place in heaven before the kingdom of God where Satan attempts to question the integrity of Job, a righteous man. We see the "sons of God", an expression to designate the angels, who come to present their reports. Satan, the adversary, also presents himself among them. When God asks him if he has seen Job, a man of integrity and righteousness, who fears God and flees evil, Satan challenges Job's sincerity, arguing that his devotion and his integrity are conditional on the protection that his riches provide him. Satan claims that if God takes away his possessions, Job will curse Him to His face. Trusting in Job's sincerity and integrity, God allows Satan to take everything that belongs to him while preserving his life. Through a series of catastrophic events, Job loses all his possessions and his children in a single day.

2. **Job 2:1-7**

1 Again there was a day when the sons of God came to present themselves before the Lord, and Satan came also among them to present himself before the Lord.

2 And the Lord said unto Satan, From whence comest thou? And Satan answered the Lord, and said, From going to and fro in the earth, and from walking up and down in it.

3 And the Lord said unto Satan, Hast thou considered my servant Job, that there is none like him in the earth, a perfect and an upright man, one that feareth God, and escheweth evil? and still he holdeth fast his integrity, although thou movedst me against him, to destroy him without cause.

4 And Satan answered the Lord, and said, Skin for skin, yea, all that a man hath will he give for his life.

5 But put forth thine hand now, and touch his bone and his flesh, and he will curse thee to thy face.

6 And the Lord said unto Satan, Behold, he is in thine hand; but save his life.

7 So went Satan forth from the presence of the Lord, and smote Job with sore boils from the sole of his foot unto his crown.

Summary

Once again, Satan appears before God in the midst of the "sons of God." Again, God asks him if he has seen Job, maintaining his initial remarks about him, namely that he is an honest and upright man who fears God and flees evil, and mentioning that he remains firm in his integrity despite having lost everything. Thereupon, Satan argues that if Job were to suffer physically, he would certainly curse God, thereby meaning that Job's good physical health is the thread that still holds him together. Once again, God allows Satan to attack Job by attacking his physical health while insisting that he preserve his life. Thereupon, Satan inflicts painful wounds on Job that cover him from head to toe. As a response to his suffering, Job sits on ashes and uses a shard to scrape his wounds.

3. **Job 4:17-19**

17 Shall mortal man be more just than God? shall a man be more pure than his maker?

18 Behold, he put no trust in his servants; and his angels he charged with folly:

19 How much less in them that dwell in houses of clay, whose foundation is in the dust, which are crushed before the moth?

Summary

Eliphaz, one of Job's friends, trying to comfort him in his suffering, suggests that even angels, who are divine beings, are not without fault in God's eyes. He emphasizes the idea that humans, being even less perfect than angels, should not expect to be considered blameless by God.

Chapter 9
Angels in the Book of Psalms

1. **Psalm 8:4-6**

   4 What is man, that thou art mindful of him? and the son of man, that thou visitest him?

   5 For thou hast made him a little lower than the angels, and hast crowned him with glory and honour.

   6 Thou madest him to have dominion over the works of thy hands; thou hast put all things under his feet:

   Summary

   These verses express the psalmist's awe and wonder at the majesty and greatness of God, especially in contrast to humanity's seemingly insignificant position in the universe. The psalmist marvels that, despite the apparent insignificance of humanity, God cares for them and has crowned them with glory and honor, giving them dominion over the works of his hands.

2. Psalm 18:10

And he rode upon a cherub, and did fly: yea, he did fly upon the wings of the wind.

Summary

This text presents a situation where the psalmist finds himself in a moment of distress and danger and calls upon God to help him. It describes God's quick, immediate, and violent reaction and accompanying anger as He comes to the psalmist's aid. Nature trembles under His passage as He moves, riding on a cherub and soaring on the wings of the wind.

3. Psalm 34:7

The angel of the LORD encampeth round about them that fear him, and delivereth them.

Summary

In this verse, the psalmist expresses the idea that God's protection extends to those who respect and fear him. The image of the angel of the Lord camping around these people translates to divine protection and deliverance from danger.

4. Psalm 35:5-6

5 Let them be as chaff before the wind: and let the angel of the LORD chase them.

6 Let their way be dark and slippery: and let the angel of the LORD persecute them.

All Angels in the Bible

Summary

In these verses, the psalmist implores God to help him and intervene against the enemies who seek to harm him unjustly. He describes them as evil adversaries, having evil intentions toward him and setting traps and pursuing him for no reason. He prays that they will be scattered and driven away like worthless chaff blown by the wind, only to have their path become treacherous and uncertain with the angel of the Lord in pursuit. They ask for God's intervention to thwart their plans against him.

5. **Psalm 68:17**

The chariots of God are twenty thousand, even thousands of angels: the Lord is among them, as in Sinai, in the holy place.

Summary

In this verse, the psalmist describes an escort of God with thousands of heavenly chariots and innumerable angels or heavenly beings. God stands in the middle of this spectacle as on Mount Sinai, where He manifested himself to the children of Israel with thunder, lightning, earthquakes, clouds, fire, and smoke. This imagery emphasizes the immense power and majesty of God.

6. **Psalm 78:25**

Man did eat angels' food: he sent them meat to the full.

Summary

The psalmist reflects on a miraculous event in the history of the Israelites when they received the "bread of angels" as food, in this case, manna, during their journey in the desert, which God provided them in abundance during their difficult times.

7. Psalm 78:49

He cast upon them the fierceness of his anger, wrath, and indignation, and trouble, by sending evil angels among them.

Summary

In this verse, the psalmist describes how God proceeded to overcome Egypt and bring out the children of Israel. It highlights the anger, fury, rage, indignation, and distress that God unleashed on Egypt through the angels of doom or destroyers that He ordained.

8. Psalm 80:1

(To the chief Musician upon Shoshannimeduth, A Psalm of Asaph.) Give ear, O Shepherd of Israel, thou that leadest Joseph like a flock; thou that dwellest between the cherubims, shine forth.

Summary

In this verse, the psalmist addresses God as the shepherd of Israel, recognizing his role as protector and guide of the people, just as a shepherd cares for his flock. The expression "enthroned over the cherubim" refers to the celestial and majestic nature of God.

9. Psalm 91:11

For he shall give his angels charge over thee, to keep thee in all thy ways.

Summary

This text indicates that God will send his angels to watch over and protect those who trust in him. It expresses the belief that God's divine intervention and protection are available to those who have faith and seek His refuge.

10. Psalm 99:1

The LORD reigneth; let the people tremble: he sitteth between the cherubims; let the earth be moved.

Summary

The verse begins with the psalmist's declaration that the Lord reigns, indicating His supreme authority and rule over all. He then describes God sitting enthroned on the cherubim, emphasizing his celestial and majestic presence.

11. Psalm 103:20

Bless the LORD, ye his angels, that excel in strength, that do his commandments, hearkening unto the voice of his word.

Summary

In this verse, the psalmist calls on the angels to praise and bless God. It identifies angels as powerful beings who faithfully carry out God's commandments and obey the voice of His word. This, therefore, highlights their devotion and obedience to God.

12. Psalm 104:4

Who maketh his angels spirits; his ministers a flaming fire:

Summary

Here, the psalmist highlights God's superpower and sovereignty over both the natural and spiritual worlds. The presence of angels refers to the spiritual world. The verse describes how God is able to control everything natural as well as spiritual.

13. Psalm 148:2

Praise ye him, all his angels: praise ye him, all his hosts.

Summary

Here, as the psalmist praises God for who He is, he invites all the angels and heavenly beings to accompany him in offering praise and worship to the Lord.

Chapter 10
Angels in the Book of Ecclesiastes

1. **Ecclesiastes 5:6**

   Suffer not thy mouth to cause thy flesh to sin; neither say thou before the angel, that it was an error: wherefore should God be angry at thy voice, and destroy the work of thine hands?

   Summary

   In this verse, the author advises against making hasty vows or promises to God and then retracting them and trying to apologize later, claiming it was a mistake. He warns those who do this that they can provoke God's anger against them since an angel pays attention to what we say.

Chapter 11
Angels in the Book of Isaiah

1. **Isaiah 6:1-6**

   1 Above it stood the seraphims: each one had six wings; with twain he covered his face, and with twain he covered his feet, and with twain he did fly.

   2 Above it stood the seraphims: each one had six wings; with twain he covered his face, and with twain he covered his feet, and with twain he did fly.

   3 And one cried unto another, and said, Holy, holy, holy, is the Lord of hosts: the whole earth is full of his glory.

   4 And the posts of the door moved at the voice of him that cried, and the house was filled with smoke.

   5 Then said I, Woe is me! for I am undone; because I am a man of unclean lips, and I dwell in the midst of a people of unclean lips: for mine eyes have seen the King, the Lord of hosts.

   6 Then flew one of the seraphims unto me, having a live coal in his hand, which he had taken with the tongs from off the altar:

All Angels in the Bible

Summary

In this passage, Isaiah recounts a powerful vision he had in the year of King Uzziah's death, where he saw the Lord seated on a throne in the heavenly temple, high and exalted—images that reflect the majesty and glory of God. He is the first to see seraphim, and he describes how they work. He explains how, by declaring the holiness of God, at the voice of these beings, the foundations of the celestial temple tremble—as if to convince those who were not convinced of the power of these angels. The temple is filled with smoke, signifying the presence of God. Faced with such a spectacle, Isaiah expresses his unworthiness and that of his people, mentioning that he has impure lips and that he lives among people with impure lips. One of the seraphim purifies his lips with a burning coal taken from the altar. He then hears the voice of the Lord asking who he will send as his messenger, and Isaiah volunteers to be God's messenger.

2. Isaiah 37:16

O LORD of hosts, God of Israel, that dwellest between the cherubims, thou art the God, even thou alone, of all the kingdoms of the earth: thou hast made heaven and earth.

Summary

In this verse, Hezekiah, king of Judah, calls upon the God of Israel, who dwells among the cherubim. The context is particular since his kingdom is besieged by the powerful army of Assyria, against which his army is powerless. He recognizes that, in this situation, only God can help him.

3. **Isaiah 37:36**

   Then the angel of the LORD went forth, and smote in the camp of the Assyrians a hundred and fourscore and five thousand: and when they arose early in the morning, behold, they were all dead corpses.

   Summary

   This text describes the miraculous deliverance brought by God in response to King Hezekiah's prayer by sending a single angel, in one night, to kill no fewer than 185,000 Assyrian soldiers. This causes King Sennacherib to withdraw in shame to Nineveh, where he will be assassinated by two of his sons inside the temple of his god, in whom he placed all his trust.

4. **Isaiah 63:9**

   In all their affliction he was afflicted, and the angel of his presence saved them: in his love and in his pity he redeemed them; and he bare them, and carried them all the days of old.

   Summary

   The prophet Isaiah recounts God's sensitivity to the times of trouble and suffering of Israel, the compassion he showed toward them, and how he sent the angel of his presence to deliver them. This divine intervention expresses God's love and mercy toward his people.

Chapter 12
Angels in the Book of Ezekiel

1. Ezekiel 1:4-28

4 And I looked, and, behold, a whirlwind came out of the north, a great cloud, and a fire infolding itself, and a brightness was about it, and out of the midst thereof as the colour of amber, out of the midst of the fire.

5 Also out of the midst thereof came the likeness of four living creatures. And this was their appearance; they had the likeness of a man.

6 And every one had four faces, and every one had four wings.

7 And their feet were straight feet; and the sole of their feet was like the sole of a calf's foot: and they sparkled like the colour of burnished brass.

8 And they had the hands of a man under their wings on their four sides; and they four had their faces and their wings.

9 Their wings were joined one to another; they turned not when they went; they went every one straight forward.

10 As for the likeness of their faces, they four had the face of a man, and the face of a lion, on the right side: and they four had the face of an ox on the left side; they four also had the face of an eagle.

11 Thus were their faces: and their wings were stretched upward; two wings of every one were joined one to another, and two covered their bodies.

12 And they went every one straight forward: whither the spirit was to go, they went; and they turned not when they went.

13 As for the likeness of the living creatures, their appearance was like burning coals of fire, and like the appearance of lamps: it went up and down among the living creatures; and the fire was bright, and out of the fire went forth lightning.

14 And the living creatures ran and returned as the appearance of a flash of lightning.

15 Now as I beheld the living creatures, behold one wheel upon the earth by the living creatures, with his four faces.

16 The appearance of the wheels and their work was like unto the colour of a beryl: and they four had one likeness: and their appearance and their work was as it were a wheel in the middle of a wheel.

17 When they went, they went upon their four sides: and they turned not when they went.

18 As for their rings, they were so high that they were dreadful; and their rings were full of eyes round about them four.

19 And when the living creatures went, the wheels went by them: and when the living creatures were lifted up from the earth, the wheels were lifted up.

20 Whithersoever the spirit was to go, they went, thither was their spirit to go; and the wheels were lifted up over against them: for the spirit of the living creature was in the wheels.

21 When those went, these went; and when those stood, these stood; and when those were lifted up from the earth, the wheels were lifted up over against them: for the spirit of the living creature was in the wheels.

22 And the likeness of the firmament upon the heads of the living creature was as the colour of the terrible crystal, stretched forth over their heads above.

23 And under the firmament were their wings straight, the one toward the other: every one had two, which covered on this side, and every one had two, which covered on that side, their bodies.

24 And when they went, I heard the noise of their wings, like the noise of great waters, as the voice of the Almighty, the voice of speech, as the noise of an host: when they stood, they let down their wings.

25 And there was a voice from the firmament that was over their heads, when they stood, and had let down their wings.

26 And above the firmament that was over their heads was the likeness of a throne, as the appearance of a sapphire stone: and upon the likeness of the throne was the likeness as the appearance of a man above upon it.

27 And I saw as the colour of amber, as the appearance of fire round about within it, from the appearance of his loins even upward, and from the appearance of his loins even downward, I saw as it were the appearance of fire, and it had brightness round about.

28 As the appearance of the bow that is in the cloud in the day of rain, so was the appearance of the brightness round about. This was the appearance of the likeness of the glory of the Lord. And when I saw it, I fell upon my face, and I heard a voice of one that spake.

Summary

In this passage, Ezekiel presents us with his vision of the four living beings who come to him in a setting of great storm wind, cloud, fire, and light. He describes them as having four faces: that of a human, a lion, an ox, and an eagle. They each had four wings, feet like those of a calf, and an appearance like burning coals. They did not turn because each could walk straight ahead, and their movement was rapid and coordinated. Above these beings, he sees an object that looks like a throne that sparkles like crystal, on which is a human figure that looks like shiny metal. These creatures move in harmony with their minds without turning around as they go.

2. Ezekiel 9:1-3

1 He cried also in mine ears with a loud voice, saying, Cause them that have charge over the city to draw near, even every man with his destroying weapon in his hand.

2 And, behold, six men came from the way of the higher gate, which lieth toward the north, and every man a slaughter weapon in his hand; and one man among them was clothed with linen, with a writer's inkhorn by his side: and they went in, and stood beside the brasen altar.

3 And the glory of the God of Israel was gone up from the cherub, whereupon he was, to the threshold of the house. And he called to the man clothed with linen, which had the writer's inkhorn by his side;

Summary

In this passage, the prophet Ezekiel has a vision in which he sees a group of six men, including one dressed in linen, mortally armed, who enter the city of Jerusalem with the mission of destroying the city. The man dressed in linen, for his part, is responsible for going through the city and marking, as a sign of protection, the foreheads of all those who sigh and lament because of the abominations and sins that occur there. God commands men to do no harm to anyone who has the mark but that they may strike anyone who does not have it. To make matters worse, the glory of God in the temple, the symbol of divine presence and protection among the people, was removed from its place near the cherubim.

3. Ezekiel 10:1-22

1 Then I looked, and, behold, in the firmament that was above the head of the cherubims there appeared over them as it were a sapphire stone, as the appearance of the likeness of a throne.

2 And he spake unto the man clothed with linen, and said, Go in between the wheels, even under the cherub, and fill thine hand with coals of fire from between the cherubims, and scatter them over the city. And he went in in my sight.

3 Now the cherubims stood on the right side of the house, when the man went in; and the cloud filled the inner court.

4 Then the glory of the LORD went up from the cherub, and stood over the threshold of the house; and the house was filled with the cloud, and the court was full of the brightness of the LORD'S glory.

5 And the sound of the cherubims' wings was heard even to the outer court, as the voice of the Almighty God when he speaketh.

6 And it came to pass, that when he had commanded the man clothed with linen, saying, Take fire from between the wheels, from between the cherubims; then he went in, and stood beside the wheels.

7 And one cherub stretched forth his hand from between the cherubims unto the fire that was between the cherubims, and took thereof, and put it into the hands of him that was clothed with linen: who took it, and went out.

8 And there appeared in the cherubims the form of a man's hand under their wings.

9 And when I looked, behold the four wheels by the cherubims, one wheel by one cherub, and another wheel by another cherub: and the appearance of the wheels was as the colour of a beryl stone.

10 And as for their appearances, they four had one likeness, as if a wheel had been in the midst of a wheel.

11 When they went, they went upon their four sides; they turned not as they went, but to the place whither the head looked they followed it; they turned not as they went.

12 And their whole body, and their backs, and their hands, and their wings, and the wheels, were full of eyes round about, even the wheels that they four had.

13 As for the wheels, it was cried unto them in my hearing, O wheel.

14 And every one had four faces: the first face was the face of a cherub, and the second face was the face of a man, and the third the face of a lion, and the fourth the face of an eagle.

15 And the cherubims were lifted up. This is the living creature that I saw by the river of Chebar.

16 And when the cherubims went, the wheels went by them: and when the cherubims lifted up their wings to mount up from the earth, the same wheels also turned not from beside them.

17 When they stood, these stood; and when they were lifted up, these lifted up themselves also: for the spirit of the living creature was in them.

18 Then the glory of the LORD departed from off the threshold of the house, and stood over the cherubims.

19 And the cherubims lifted up their wings, and mounted up from the earth in my sight: when they went out, the wheels also were beside them, and every one stood at the door of the east gate of the LORD'S house; and the glory of the God of Israel was over them above.

20 This is the living creature that I saw under the God of Israel by the river of Chebar; and I knew that they were the cherubims.

21 Every one had four faces apiece, and every one four wings; and the likeness of the hands of a man was under their wings.

22 And the likeness of their faces was the same faces which I saw by the river of Chebar, their appearances and themselves: they went every one straight forward.

Summary

In this passage, Ezekiel continues with the vision, observing the same cherubim he had seen previously. He describes them standing next to the Temple in Jerusalem, having four faces (human, lion, ox, and eagle), and their wings touching each other, forming a protective barrier around the throne. He notices that they come with wheels, which is a complex structure with rims full of eyes. They allow them to move in any direction without turning and support the divine throne. A voice from heaven commands the cherubim to scatter coals over Jerusalem, which symbolizes the judgment and destruction of the city. The vision ends when Ezekiel observes the glory of the Lord leaving the Temple and ascending above the city, signifying God's departure from Jerusalem due to its idolatry and abominations.

4. **Ezekiel 11:22-23**

22 Then did the cherubim lift up their wings, and the wheels beside them; and the glory of the God of Israel was over them above.

23 And the glory of the Lord went up from the midst of the city, and stood upon the mountain which is on the east side of the city.

All Angels in the Bible

Summary

In this passage, the prophet Ezekiel recounts a symbolic and powerful moment in his vision. He sees the glory of the Lord, who had previously left the Temple because of the abominations of the city, returning to its place near the cherubim to rise in the middle of the city and go to the top of a mountain to the east of the city.

5. Ezekiel 28:14-16

14 Thou art the anointed cherub that covereth; and I have set thee so: thou wast upon the holy mountain of God; thou hast walked up and down in the midst of the stones of fire.

15 Thou wast perfect in thy ways from the day that thou wast created, till iniquity was found in thee.

16 By the multitude of thy merchandise they have filled the midst of thee with violence, and thou hast sinned: therefore I will cast thee as profane out of the mountain of God: and I will destroy thee, O covering cherub, from the midst of the stones of fire.

Summary

This passage about Lucifer (Satan) describes who he was (a protective cherub), where he was assigned (the holy mountain of God), and the glory he had (he walked among the sparkling stones) until the day iniquity was found in him.

6. Ezekiel 41:18-25

18 And it was made with cherubims and palm trees, so that a palm tree was between a cherub and a cherub; and every cherub had two faces;

19 So that the face of a man was toward the palm tree on the one side, and the face of a young lion toward the palm tree on the other side: it was made through all the house round about.

20 From the ground unto above the door were cherubims and palm trees made, and on the wall of the temple.

21 The posts of the temple were squared, and the face of the sanctuary; the appearance of the one as the appearance of the other.

22 The altar of wood was three cubits high, and the length thereof two cubits; and the corners thereof, and the length thereof, and the walls thereof, were of wood: and he said unto me, This is the table that is before the Lord.

23 And the temple and the sanctuary had two doors.

24 And the doors had two leaves apiece, two turning leaves; two leaves for the one door, and two leaves for the other door.

25 And there were made on them, on the doors of the temple, cherubims and palm trees, like as were made upon the walls; and there were thick planks upon the face of the porch without.

All Angels in the Bible

Summary

In this text, Ezekiel presents the details of the temple that he saw in his vision, as well as the relative measurements. Thus, we find information on the woodwork that decorated the interior walls of the temple carved with cherubim, the interior sanctuary named "Debir," the walls of the temple, the exterior sanctuary, and the doors also covered with sculptures of cherubim.

Chapter 13
Angels in the Book of Daniel

1. Daniel 3:28

Then Nebuchadnezzar spake, and said, Blessed be the God of Shadrach, Meshach, and Abednego, who hath sent his angel, and delivered his servants that trusted in him, and have changed the king's word, and yielded their bodies, that they might not serve nor worship any god, except their own God.

Summary

In this verse, King Nebuchadnezzar of Babylon publicly acknowledges the faith and loyalty of Shadrach, Meshach, and Abednego, the three Jewish men who refused to worship his statue. Thrown into a fiery furnace as punishment for their refusal, an angel of God protected them from the fire so that they emerged unscathed without their clothes being burned by the flames. Faced with this miracle, the king was amazed and recognized that God had sent his angel to protect them and deliver them from the furnace. He reversed his decision and had a decree published throughout the kingdom prohibiting anyone from speaking ill of the God of Shadrach, Meshach, and Abednego, because there is no other god who can deliver like Him.

2. **Daniel 6:22**

My God hath sent his angel, and hath shut the lions' mouths, that they have not hurt me: forasmuch as before him innocency was found in me; and also before thee, O king, have I done no hurt.

Summary

King Darius, after reluctantly ordering Daniel to be thrown into the lions' den to fulfill the decree he had been led to sign, goes to the den early in the morning. To his great astonishment, he finds Daniel alive and without any trace of injury among the lions. Noticing his astonishment, Daniel informs him that God had sent his angel and closed the lions' mouths because he was innocent. The king rejoices and recognizes the miraculous intervention of Daniel's God to spare his life.

Chapter 14
Angels in the Book of Hosea

1. **Hosea 12:4**

   Yea, he had power over the angel, and prevailed: he wept, and made supplication unto him: he found him in Bethel, and there he spake with us;

   Summary

   In this verse, the prophet Hosea recalls the story of Jacob when he wrestled with an angel and how he wept and sought God's favor. The text highlights Jacob's perseverance and humility as he sought God's blessing and forgiveness.

Chapter 15
Angels in the Book of Zechariah

1. **Zechariah 1:9-19**

   9 Then said I, O my lord, what are these? And the angel that talked with me said unto me, I will shew thee what these be.

   10 And the man that stood among the myrtle trees answered and said, These are they whom the Lord hath sent to walk to and fro through the earth.

   11 And they answered the angel of the LORD that stood among the myrtle trees, and said, We have walked to and fro through the earth, and, behold, all the earth sitteth still, and is at rest.

   12 Then the angel of the LORD answered and said, O LORD of hosts, how long wilt thou not have mercy on Jerusalem and on the cities of Judah, against which thou hast had indignation these threescore and ten years?

   13 And the LORD answered the angel that talked with me with good words and comfortable words.

   14 So the angel that communed with me said unto me, Cry thou, saying, Thus saith the LORD of hosts;

I am jealous for Jerusalem and for Zion with a great jealousy.

15 And I am very sore displeased with the heathen that are at ease: for I was but a little displeased, and they helped forward the affliction.

16 Therefore thus saith the Lord; I am returned to Jerusalem with mercies: my house shall be built in it, saith the Lord of hosts, and a line shall be stretched forth upon Jerusalem.

17 Cry yet, saying, Thus saith the Lord of hosts; My cities through prosperity shall yet be spread abroad; and the Lord shall yet comfort Zion, and shall yet choose Jerusalem.

18 And I said unto the angel that talked with me, What be these? And he answered me, These are the horns which have scattered Judah, Israel, and Jerusalem.

19 And I said unto the angel that talked with me, What be these? And he answered me, These are the horns which have scattered Judah, Israel, and Jerusalem.

Summary

Zechariah receives a night vision from the Lord in which he sees a man riding a red horse among the myrtles. He asks the meaning of this vision, and an angel responds that these horses represent those the Lord has sent to patrol the earth. The man on the red horse reports to the Lord that the earth is at rest and quiet, and he asks Him when He will show mercy to Jerusalem and the cities of Judah. The Lord responds with comforting words to Zechariah and the people, expressing his jealousy for Jerusalem and his anger against the nations who oppressed Israel. He promises to return to Jerusalem with mercy and rebuild the city, ensuring its future prosperity and restoration.

2. Zechariah 2:3-5

3 And, behold, the angel that talked with me went forth, and another angel went out to meet him,

4 And said unto him, Run, speak to this young man, saying, Jerusalem shall be inhabited as towns without walls for the multitude of men and cattle therein:

5 For I, saith the Lord, will be unto her a wall of fire round about, and will be the glory in the midst of her.

Summary

The interpreting angel informs Zechariah that another angel is coming with a line to measure the city of Jerusalem. Zechariah is informed that Jerusalem will be a city without walls due to the multitude of people and livestock there. The Lord himself will be a wall of fire around Jerusalem and the glory that is there.

3. Zechariah 3:1-7

1 And he shewed me Joshua the high priest standing before the angel of the LORD, and Satan standing at his right hand to resist him.

2 And the Lord said unto Satan, The Lord rebuke thee, O Satan; even the Lord that hath chosen Jerusalem rebuke thee: is not this a brand plucked out of the fire?

3 Now Joshua was clothed with filthy garments, and stood before the angel.

4 And he answered and spake unto those that stood before him, saying, Take away the filthy garments from him. And unto him he said, Behold, I have caused thine iniquity to pass from thee, and I will clothe thee with change of raiment.

5 And I said, Let them set a fair mitre upon his head. So they set a fair mitre upon his head, and clothed him with garments. And the angel of the LORD stood by.

6 And the angel of the LORD protested unto Joshua, saying,

7 Thus saith the Lord of hosts; If thou wilt walk in my ways, and if thou wilt keep my charge, then thou shalt also judge my house, and shalt also keep my courts, and I will give thee places to walk among these that stand by.

All Angels in the Bible

Summary

Zechariah has a vision in which Joshua, the High Priest, is accused by Satan (the accuser) in the presence of the angel of the Lord. The Lord defends him by rebuking Satan and reminding him that Joshua is a brand plucked from the fire, thus showing mercy and protection toward him. Joshua is dressed in dirty clothes, symbolizing his sin and impurity, but the Lord commands those standing before him to remove these clothes. Then he is given rich garments to wear, symbolizing the passage from impurity to righteousness and a clean turban is placed on his head. The angel of the Lord proclaims that Joshua and his fellow priests are a sign of things to come and that God will take away Joshua's iniquity. The angel of the Lord declared to him that if he walks in the ways of God and respects his office as priest, he will judge the house of God and have access to his presence.

4. Zechariah 4:1-5

1 And the angel that talked with me came again, and waked me, as a man that is wakened out of his sleep,

2 And said unto me, What seest thou? And I said, I have looked, and behold a candlestick all of gold, with a bowl upon the top of it, and his seven lamps thereon, and seven pipes to the seven lamps, which are upon the top thereof:

3 And two olive trees by it, one upon the right side of the bowl, and the other upon the left side thereof.

4 So I answered and spake to the angel that talked with me, saying, What are these, my lord?

5 Then the angel that talked with me answered and said unto me, Knowest thou not what these be? And I said, No, my lord.

Summary

Zechariah sees a vision of a golden lampstand with a vase on top and seven lamps on it. There are also seven conduits to the lamps, with two olive trees, one on the right side of the vase and the other on the left. Zechariah questions the angel who spoke to him about the meaning of the vision, and he explains that the vision symbolizes the word of the Lord to Zerubbabel (the governor of Judah), conveying the message: "It is not by might nor by power, but by my spirit, saith the LORD of hosts."

5. Zechariah 5:5-11

5 Then the angel that talked with me went forth, and said unto me, Lift up now thine eyes, and see what is this that goeth forth.

6 And I said, What is it? And he said, This is an ephah that goeth forth. He said moreover, This is their resemblance through all the earth.

7 And, behold, there was lifted up a talent of lead: and this is a woman that sitteth in the midst of the ephah.

8 And he said, This is wickedness. And he cast it into the midst of the ephah; and he cast the weight of lead upon the mouth thereof.

9 Then lifted I up mine eyes, and looked, and, behold, there came out two women, and the wind was in their wings; for they had wings like the wings of a stork: and they lifted up the ephah between the earth and the heaven.

10 Then said I to the angel that talked with me, Whither do these bear the ephah?

11 And he said unto me, To build it an house in the land of Shinar: and it shall be established, and set there upon her own base.

Summary

In this passage, Zechariah shares with us a vision in which he observes a flying scroll. The angel informs him that the scroll represents a curse spreading over the land, entering the homes of thieves and those who swear falsely by the name of the Lord. Once in the houses, the scroll consumes the wood and stones as a sign of divine judgment, leading to the destruction of the unjust. In another vision, Zechariah sees a woman, representing wickedness, who is placed in a basket covered with lead. It is described as being thrown into the middle of an ephah, which is a dry unit of measurement. Then two women with wings lift the ephah measure containing the wicked woman into the sky between heaven and earth. Zechariah inquires about the meaning of this vision, and the angel explains that the ephah represents wickedness, and the two women with wings take the measure of the ephah to build him a house in the land of Shinar.

6. Zechariah 6:1-8

1 Then I answered and said unto the angel that talked with me, What are these, my lord?

2 In the first chariot were red horses; and in the second chariot black horses;

3 And in the third chariot white horses; and in the fourth chariot grisled and bay horses.

4 Then I answered and said unto the angel that talked with me, What are these, my lord?

5 And the angel answered and said unto me, These are the four spirits of the heavens, which go forth from standing before the Lord of all the earth.

6 The black horses which are therein go forth into the north country; and the white go forth after them; and the grisled go forth toward the south country.

7 And the bay went forth, and sought to go that they might walk to and fro through the earth: and he said, Get you hence, walk to and fro through the earth. So they walked to and fro through the earth.

8 Then cried he upon me, and spake unto me, saying, Behold, these that go toward the north country have quieted my spirit in the north country.

All Angels in the Bible

Summary

In another vision, Zechariah sees four chariots emerging from between two bronze mountains. Each chariot is pulled by different horses: red, black, white, and spotted. Asking the meaning of this vision, an angel explains that these are the four winds of heaven, which come out from the place where they stood before the Lord of all the earth. Chariots are sent by the Lord to patrol the earth, signifying His watchful presence and control over the entire world. Zechariah is instructed to take silver and gold, make a crown, and place it on the head of Joshua, the high priest. This is a symbolic act indicating the combination of priestly and royal roles. Zechariah is also responsible for telling Joshua that he will be a priest on the throne and that there will be harmony and cooperation between the priestly and royal roles.

7. Zechariah 12:8

In that day shall the LORD defend the inhabitants of Jerusalem; and he that is feeble among them at that day shall be as David; and the house of David shall be as God, as the angel of the LORD before them.

Summary

In this verse, the prophet Zechariah speaks of a future time when the Lord will defend the inhabitants of Jerusalem. He declares that on that day, the Lord will protect the people of Jerusalem and that even the weakest among them will be as strong as David, the famous king of Israel, because the angel of the Lord will go before them.

Chapter 16
Angels in the Book of Matthew

1. **Matthew 1:20**

   But while he thought on these things, behold, the angel of the Lord appeared unto him in a dream, saying, Joseph, thou son of David, fear not to take unto thee Mary thy wife: for that which is conceived in her is of the Holy Ghost.

   Summary

   In a dream, an angel of the Lord appeared to Joseph, who was engaged to Mary, to reassure him about her pregnancy by saying to him, "Joseph, son of David, do not be afraid to take Mary as your wife, for what is conceived in it comes from the Holy Spirit."

2. **Matthew 1:24**

   Then Joseph being raised from sleep did as the angel of the Lord had bidden him, and took unto him his wife:

   Summary

   Joseph obeyed the angel's instructions after he explained the divine origin of Mary's pregnancy. He takes her as his wife, demonstrating his faith and obedience to God's plan.

3. Matthew 2:13-15

13 And when they were departed, behold, the angel of the Lord appeareth to Joseph in a dream, saying, Arise, and take the young child and his mother, and flee into Egypt, and be thou there until I bring thee word: for Herod will seek the young child to destroy him.

14 When he arose, he took the young child and his mother by night, and departed into Egypt:

15 And was there until the death of Herod: that it might be fulfilled which was spoken of the Lord by the prophet, saying, Out of Egypt have I called my son.

Summary

In a dream, Joseph was warned to take Mary and the child and flee to Egypt following the visit of the wise men who had come to worship Jesus. The angel explains that King Herod is trying to kill the child. Joseph obeys the angel's command and takes Mary and young Jesus to Egypt to escape Herod's threat. They remain there until Herod's death, fulfilling a prophecy that says, "I have called my son out of Egypt."

4. Matthew 2:19-21

19 But when Herod was dead, behold, an angel of the Lord appeareth in a dream to Joseph in Egypt,

20 Saying, Arise, and take the young child and his mother, and go into the land of Israel: for they are dead which sought the young child's life.

21 And he arose, and took the young child and his mother, and came into the land of Israel.

Summary

While in Egypt, Joseph is warned in a dream of the death of King Herod. The angel tells him to take Mary and Jesus and return to Israel because those who wanted to take the child's life were now dead. Joseph obeys the angel's command and takes his family back to Israel.

5. **Matthew 4:6-11**

6 And saith unto him, If thou be the Son of God, cast thyself down: for it is written, He shall give his angels charge concerning thee: and in their hands they shall bear thee up, lest at any time thou dash thy foot against a stone.

7 Jesus said unto him, It is written again, Thou shalt not tempt the Lord thy God.

8 Again, the devil taketh him up into an exceeding high mountain, and sheweth him all the kingdoms of the world, and the glory of them;

9 And saith unto him, All these things will I give thee, if thou wilt fall down and worship me.

10 Then saith Jesus unto him, Get thee hence, Satan: for it is written, Thou shalt worship the Lord thy God, and him only shalt thou serve.

11 Then the devil leaveth him, and, behold, angels came and ministered unto him.

Summary

Citing Scripture, Satan tempts Jesus by asking him to throw himself from the temple, suggesting that the angels will save him and prevent him from harm. Jesus responds by quoting Scripture, saying, "You shall not put the Lord your God to the test."

He then takes Jesus to a high mountain and shows him all the kingdoms of the world and their splendor, offering to give them to him if he will worship him. Jesus firmly rebukes Satan, saying, "Begone, Satan! For it is written: "You shall worship the Lord your God, and him only shall you serve." With that, Satan leaves and angels come to serve Jesus.

6. Matthew 13:39-50

39 The enemy that sowed them is the devil; the harvest is the end of the world; and the reapers are the angels.

40 As therefore the tares are gathered and burned in the fire; so shall it be in the end of this world.

41 The Son of man shall send forth his angels, and they shall gather out of his kingdom all things that offend, and them which do iniquity;

42 And shall cast them into a furnace of fire: there shall be wailing and gnashing of teeth.

43 Then shall the righteous shine forth as the sun in the kingdom of their Father. Who hath ears to hear, let him hear.

44 Again, the kingdom of heaven is like unto treasure hid in a field; the which when a man hath found, he hideth, and for joy thereof goeth and selleth all that he hath, and buyeth that field.

45 Again, the kingdom of heaven is like unto a merchant man, seeking goodly pearls:

46 Who, when he had found one pearl of great price, went and sold all that he had, and bought it.

47 Again, the kingdom of heaven is like unto a net, that was cast into the sea, and gathered of every kind:

48 Which, when it was full, they drew to shore, and sat down, and gathered the good into vessels, but cast the bad away.

49 So shall it be at the end of the world: the angels shall come forth, and sever the wicked from among the just,

50 And shall cast them into the furnace of fire: there shall be wailing and gnashing of teeth.

Summary

Jesus explains the parable of the weeds to his disciples. He compares the field to the world and the good seeds to the children of the kingdom, while the weed represents the sons of evil. The enemy who sowed the weeds is the devil, and the harvest represents the end times. Jesus explains that at the end of time, the angels will gather the wicked (the weeds) and separate them from the righteous (the wheat). The wicked will be thrown into the fiery furnace, where there will be weeping and gnashing of teeth.

7. **Matthew 16:27**

For the Son of man shall come in the glory of his Father with his angels; and then he shall reward every man according to his works.

Summary

This verse emphasizes several key points, such as:

- The "Son of Man," which refers to Jesus, who will return in the future with his angels

- The return of Jesus, which will be accompanied by the glory of his Father, indicating a majestic and divine appearance

- At the time of his return, Jesus will judge each individual based on their actions and deeds. People will be rewarded according to their actions.

8. **Matthew 18:10**

Take heed that ye despise not one of these little ones; for I say unto you, That in heaven their angels do always behold the face of my Father which is in heaven.

Summary

This verse highlights the importance of valuing and protecting children. Jesus warns against looking down on them or harming them. He says that they have guardian angels watching over them who are in the presence of God constantly. It conveys the message of God's care for children and vulnerable people and of His expectation that His followers will show them love, compassion, and protection.

9. Matthew 22:30

For in the resurrection they neither marry, nor are given in marriage, but are as the angels of God in heaven.

Summary

The Sadducees, who do not believe in the resurrection, come to question Jesus about marital relations after death. Jesus answers that in the resurrection, there will be no marriage, for those who are resurrected will be like angels.

10. Matthew 24:31-36

31 And he shall send his angels with a great sound of a trumpet, and they shall gather together his elect from the four winds, from one end of heaven to the other.

32 Now learn a parable of the fig tree; When his branch is yet tender, and putteth forth leaves, ye know that summer is nigh:

33 So likewise ye, when ye shall see all these things, know that it is near, even at the doors.

34 Verily I say unto you, This generation shall not pass, till all these things be fulfilled.

35 Heaven and earth shall pass away, but my words shall not pass away.

36 But of that day and hour knoweth no man, no, not the angels of heaven, but my Father only.

Summary

Jesus describes the moment of his return when angels will be sent by a trumpet call to gather his elect from the four corners of the earth. Jesus indicates that just as the budding of the fig tree announces summer, there are clear signs announcing that his return is near. He assures his disciples that "this generation will not pass away until all these things come to pass," implying that some of those living at the time were the first witnesses to these events.

Jesus also emphasizes that no one knows the exact day or hour of his return, neither the angels nor himself, but only the Father.

11. Matthew 25:31-41

31 When the Son of man shall come in his glory, and all the holy angels with him, then shall he sit upon the throne of his glory:

32 And before him shall be gathered all nations: and he shall separate them one from another, as a shepherd divideth his sheep from the goats:

33 And he shall set the sheep on his right hand, but the goats on the left.

34 Then shall the King say unto them on his right hand, Come, ye blessed of my Father, inherit the kingdom prepared for you from the foundation of the world:

35 For I was an hungred, and ye gave me meat: I was thirsty, and ye gave me drink: I was a stranger, and ye took me in:

36 Naked, and ye clothed me: I was sick, and ye visited me: I was in prison, and ye came unto me.

37 Then shall the righteous answer him, saying, Lord, when saw we thee an hungred, and fed thee? or thirsty, and gave thee drink?

38 When saw we thee a stranger, and took thee in? or naked, and clothed thee?

39 Or when saw we thee sick, or in prison, and came unto thee?

40 And the King shall answer and say unto them, Verily I say unto you, Inasmuch as ye have done it unto one of the least of these my brethren, ye have done it unto me.

41 Then shall he say also unto them on the left hand, Depart from me, ye cursed, into everlasting fire, prepared for the devil and his angels:

Summary

In this text, Jesus describes a scene of the last judgment where the Son of Man comes in his glory, escorted by all the angels. He will sit on the throne of his glory to judge the nations who will be assembled before him. He will begin by sorting by separating the righteous, compared to sheep, who are placed on his right, from the unrighteous, who are compared to goats and placed on his left. The righteous are praised for their actions toward Jesus and have inherited the kingdom, while the unrighteous are reprimanded and cursed for the same reasons. The righteous are surprised and ask Jesus when they saw him hungry, thirsty, a stranger, naked, sick, or in prison. Jesus responds by saying that when they did these things for the least of his brothers and sisters, they were doing them for him. The unjust ask him the same question, and Jesus answers that when they did not do these things for the least of his brothers and sisters, they did not do them for him.

12. Matthew 26:53

Thinkest thou that I cannot now pray to my Father, and he shall presently give me more than twelve legions of angels?

Summary

Wanting to oppose the arrest of Jesus, one of the disciples drew his sword, struck the servant of the high priest, and cut off his ear. Jesus ordered him to put his sword back in its place, reminding him that all who take the sword will also die by the sword. Then, to indicate that he was willingly allowing himself to be taken away, he informed those who came to arrest him that if he appealed to his Father, more than twelve legions of angels would be sent to his aid immediately.

13. Matthew 28:2-7

2 And, behold, there was a great earthquake: for the angel of the Lord descended from heaven, and came and rolled back the stone from the door, and sat upon it.

3 His countenance was like lightning, and his raiment white as snow:

4 And for fear of him the keepers did shake, and became as dead men.

5 And the angel answered and said unto the women, Fear not ye: for I know that ye seek Jesus, which was crucified.

6 He is not here: for he is risen, as he said. Come, see the place where the Lord lay.

7 And go quickly, and tell his disciples that he is risen from the dead; and, behold, he goeth before you into Galilee; there shall ye see him: lo, I have told you.

Summary

At dawn on the first day of the week, an earthquake is caused at the tomb of Jesus by the descent of an angel who came to roll away the stone. Trembling with fear, the guards lose consciousness. While sitting on the stone, the angel addresses Mary Magdalene and the other Mary who had gone there. After reassuring them, he informs them that Jesus is resurrected and that he is not in the tomb. Then he invites them to enter and take stock. Then he asks them to announce it to the disciples and inform them that Jesus will meet them in Galilee, as he had predicted.

Chapter 17
Angels in the Book of Mark

1. **Mark 1:13**

   And he was there in the wilderness forty days, tempted of Satan; and was with the wild beasts; and the angels ministered unto him.

   Summary

   After Jesus was baptized by John the Baptist in the Jordan River, the Holy Spirit immediately led him into the desert. There he spent forty days with the wild animals, fasting and being tempted by Satan, and the angels of God ministered to him.

2. **Mark 8:38**

   Whosoever therefore shall be ashamed of me and of my words in this adulterous and sinful generation; of him also shall the Son of man be ashamed, when he cometh in the glory of his Father with the holy angels.

   Summary

   In this verse, Jesus teaches the disciples and the crowd the importance of openly recognizing and confessing faith in Him and His teachings. He warns anyone who is ashamed of him and his words that he, too, will be ashamed of that person when he comes in glory with the angels.

3. **Mark 12:25**

   For when they shall rise from the dead, they neither marry, nor are given in marriage; but are as the angels which are in heaven.

   Summary

   Jesus explains that in the resurrection, there will be no marriage or giving in marriage. For those who have eternal life in the presence of God are like angels. This means that in heaven, the relationships between men and women as we know them on earth will be different.

4. **Mark 13:27**

   And then shall he send his angels, and shall gather together his elect from the four winds, from the uttermost part of the earth to the uttermost part of heaven.

   Summary

   Describing the future event of his return, Jesus explains that the gathering of the elect from every corner of the earth will be through angels.

5. **Mark 13:32**

   But of that day and that hour knoweth no man, no, not the angels which are in heaven, neither the Son, but the Father.

All Angels in the Bible

Summary

Responding to a question relating to the signs of his advent, Jesus takes the opportunity to explain to the disciples that, apart from the Father, no one, neither the angels of heaven nor himself, knows the exact date and hour of his return.

6. Mark 16:1-7

1 And when the sabbath was past, Mary Magdalene, and Mary the mother of James, and Salome, had bought sweet spices, that they might come and anoint him.

2 And very early in the morning the first day of the week, they came unto the sepulchre at the rising of the sun.

3 And they said among themselves, Who shall roll us away the stone from the door of the sepulchre?

4 And when they looked, they saw that the stone was rolled away: for it was very great.

5 And entering into the sepulchre, they saw a young man sitting on the right side, clothed in a long white garment; and they were affrighted.

6 And he saith unto them, Be not affrighted: Ye seek Jesus of Nazareth, which was crucified: he is risen; he is not here: behold the place where they laid him.

7 But go your way, tell his disciples and Peter that he goeth before you into Galilee: there shall ye see him, as he said unto you.

Summary

After the end of the Sabbath, Mary Magdalene, Mary, mother of James, and Salome decide to go to Jesus' tomb with spices to anoint his body. Very early, on the morning of the first day of the week, they left without knowing how they were going to roll away the large stone at the tomb entrance. Arriving just after sunrise, they found, with great astonishment, that the stone had been moved. Entering the tomb, they find, horrified, a young man dressed in a white robe who tells them not to worry and that Jesus is resurrected. Then the angel asks them to go and tell the disciples and Peter the news, that Jesus is going ahead of them to Galilee, and that he will see them there.

Chapter 18
Angels in the Book of Luke

1. **Luke 1:11-22**

   11 And there appeared unto him an angel of the Lord standing on the right side of the altar of incense.

   12 And when Zacharias saw him, he was troubled, and fear fell upon him.

   13 But the angel said unto him, Fear not, Zacharias: for thy prayer is heard; and thy wife Elisabeth shall bear thee a son, and thou shalt call his name John.

   14 And thou shalt have joy and gladness; and many shall rejoice at his birth.

   15 For he shall be great in the sight of the Lord, and shall drink neither wine nor strong drink; and he shall be filled with the Holy Ghost, even from his mother's womb.

   16 And many of the children of Israel shall he turn to the Lord their God.

   17 And he shall go before him in the spirit and power of Elias, to turn the hearts of the fathers to the children, and the disobedient to the wisdom of

the just; to make ready a people prepared for the Lord.

18 And Zacharias said unto the angel, Whereby shall I know this? for I am an old man, and my wife well stricken in years.

19 And the angel answering said unto him, I am Gabriel, that stand in the presence of God; and am sent to speak unto thee, and to shew thee these glad tidings.

20 And, behold, thou shalt be dumb, and not able to speak, until the day that these things shall be performed, because thou believest not my words, which shall be fulfilled in their season.

21 And the people waited for Zacharias, and marvelled that he tarried so long in the temple.

22 And when he came out, he could not speak unto them: and they perceived that he had seen a vision in the temple: for he beckoned unto them, and remained speechless.

Summary

The priest Zechariah, who had no children because his wife Elizabeth was barren, enters the temple to burn incense at the altar. This is a sacred and solemn duty. He is surprised and frightened by the angel Gabriel, who appears from the right side of the altar. He reassures him and tells him that his wife Elizabeth is going to give him a son, whom he must name John. He informs her that the child will bring joy and gladness, that he will be great in the eyes of the Lord, and will be filled with the Holy Spirit from his mother's womb. Having doubts, since he and his wife are already advanced in age, Zechariah asks the angel for a sign to confirm this message. As a sign, Gabriel tells him that he will no longer be able to speak until the day these things happen. When he left the temple, Zechariah could no longer speak because he was mute, and everyone understood that he had experienced something in the temple.

2. **Luke 1:26-38**

26 And in the sixth month the angel Gabriel was sent from God unto a city of Galilee, named Nazareth,

27 To a virgin espoused to a man whose name was Joseph, of the house of David; and the virgin's name was Mary.

28 And the angel came in unto her, and said, Hail, thou that art highly favoured, the Lord is with thee: blessed art thou among women.

29 And when she saw him, she was troubled at his saying, and cast in her mind what manner of salutation this should be.

30 And the angel said unto her, Fear not, Mary: for thou hast found favour with God.

31 And, behold, thou shalt conceive in thy womb, and bring forth a son, and shalt call his name Jesus.

32 He shall be great, and shall be called the Son of the Highest: and the Lord God shall give unto him the throne of his father David:

33 And he shall reign over the house of Jacob for ever; and of his kingdom there shall be no end.

34 Then said Mary unto the angel, How shall this be, seeing I know not a man?

35 And the angel answered and said unto her, The Holy Ghost shall come upon thee, and the power of the Highest shall overshadow thee: therefore also that holy thing which shall be born of thee shall be called the Son of God.

36 And, behold, thy cousin Elisabeth, she hath also conceived a son in her old age: and this is the sixth month with her, who was called barren.

37 For with God nothing shall be impossible.

38 And Mary said, Behold the handmaid of the Lord; be it unto me according to thy word. And the angel departed from her.

Summary

Sent by God to Nazareth, a town in Galilee, the angel Gabriel appears to a young virgin named Mary, betrothed to a man named Joseph, from the house of David, and greets her. After reassuring her, the angel informs her that she will conceive a child through the Holy Spirit and must name him Jesus. He will be called Son of the Most High, God will give him the throne of David, and his kingdom will have no end. After answering Mary's question about how this is going to be done, he tells her that her relative, Elizabeth, has conceived a son in her old age. Mary replies that she is the servant of the Lord and accepts that it will be done as he told her.

3. Luke 2:6-16

6 And so it was, that, while they were there, the days were accomplished that she should be delivered.

7 And she brought forth her firstborn son, and wrapped him in swaddling clothes, and laid him in a manger; because there was no room for them in the inn.

8 And there were in the same country shepherds abiding in the field, keeping watch over their flock by night.

9 And, lo, the angel of the Lord came upon them, and the glory of the Lord shone round about them: and they were sore afraid.

10 And the angel said unto them, Fear not: for, behold, I bring you good tidings of great joy, which shall be to all people.

11 For unto you is born this day in the city of David a Saviour, which is Christ the Lord.

12 And this shall be a sign unto you; Ye shall find the babe wrapped in swaddling clothes, lying in a manger.

13 And suddenly there was with the angel a multitude of the heavenly host praising God, and saying,

14 Glory to God in the highest, and on earth peace, good will toward men.

15 And it came to pass, as the angels were gone away from them into heaven, the shepherds said one to another, Let us now go even unto Bethlehem, and see this thing which is come to pass, which the Lord hath made known unto us.

16 And they came with haste, and found Mary, and Joseph, and the babe lying in a manger.

Summary

Mary and Joseph go to Bethlehem for a census. Not finding room in the inn, they find themselves in a stable where she gives birth to Jesus and then places him in a manger. An angel of the Lord appears to shepherds in the area and tells them the good news that today, in the city of David, a Savior, who is Christ, has been born and tells them where they will find the baby. A multitude of heavenly hosts suddenly appear and begin to praise God and say, "Glory to God in the highest, and on earth peace to those who please him." The shepherds go there and note the birth of Jesus, as the angel had shared with them, and decide to go and share the news with others.

4. Luke 2:21

And when eight days were accomplished for the circumcising of the child, his name was called JESUS, which was so named of the angel before he was conceived in the womb.

Summary

As was customary for Jewish male children, Mary and Joseph brought the child to be circumcised eight days after his birth and named him Jesus, as the angel had commanded.

5. Luke 4:1-10

1 And Jesus being full of the Holy Ghost returned from Jordan, and was led by the Spirit into the wilderness,

2 Being forty days tempted of the devil. And in those days he did eat nothing: and when they were ended, he afterward hungered.

3 And the devil said unto him, If thou be the Son of God, command this stone that it be made bread.

4 And Jesus answered him, saying, It is written, That man shall not live by bread alone, but by every word of God.

5 And the devil, taking him up into an high mountain, shewed unto him all the kingdoms of the world in a moment of time.

6 And the devil said unto him, All this power will I give thee, and the glory of them: for that is

delivered unto me; and to whomsoever I will I give it.

7 If thou therefore wilt worship me, all shall be thine.

8 And Jesus answered and said unto him, Get thee behind me, Satan: for it is written, Thou shalt worship the Lord thy God, and him only shalt thou serve.

9 And he brought him to Jerusalem, and set him on a pinnacle of the temple, and said unto him, If thou be the Son of God, cast thyself down from hence:

10 For it is written, He shall give his angels charge over thee, to keep thee:

Summary

Jesus, filled with the Holy Spirit, is led by the Holy Spirit into the desert, where he fasts for forty days. During this period of fasting and vulnerability, he is tempted by Satan several times. Eventually, Satan takes Jesus to the top of the temple in Jerusalem and suggests he jump because the angels will save him. Jesus responds by quoting Scripture again, saying that the Lord should not be put to the test. After these temptations, Satan moves away from him while waiting for an opportune moment.

6. Luke 9:26

For whosoever shall be ashamed of me and of my words, of him shall the Son of man be ashamed, when he shall come in his own glory, and in his Father's, and of the holy angels.

Summary

Jesus teaches his disciples that it is crucial to openly acknowledge and confess their faith in him and his teachings. He informs them that he will disapprove of anyone who is ashamed of him and his words in this world when he returns in his glory, accompanied by the glory of the Father and the angels.

7. Luke 12:8-9

8 Also I say unto you, Whosoever shall confess me before men, him shall the Son of man also confess before the angels of God:

9 But he that denieth me before men shall be denied before the angels of God.

Summary

Through these verses, Jesus emphasizes that it is important to boldly and openly recognize one's faith in Him. This underlines the idea that our recognition of Jesus before others here has a corresponding recognition of him before the heavenly hosts with God. Conversely, denying Jesus or being ashamed of him in this life will lead him to deny us before the angels with God.

8. Luke 15:10

Likewise, I say unto you, there is joy in the presence of the angels of God over one sinner that repenteth.

Summary

Jesus illustrates the great joy of angels and heavenly armies when a sinner repents and turns from his evil ways. It highlights the loving and redemptive nature of God, which celebrates the return of a lost soul to Him.

9. Luke 16:22

And it came to pass, that the beggar died, and was carried by the angels into Abraham's bosom: the rich man also died, and was buried;

Summary

This verse, taken from Jesus' parable about the rich man and poor Lazarus, contrasts the destinies of a rich man who led a joyful and brilliant life, without compassion, and a poor and sick beggar named Lazarus. After their death, Lazarus is carried by angels to Abraham's bosom, a place of comfort and rest in the afterlife, often compared to paradise. On the other hand, the rich man, who is not taken care of by the angels, is buried and finds himself in a place of torment in the afterlife. This parable warns us about the consequences of our actions and the importance of caring for others during our earthly life.

10. Luke 20:36

Neither can they die any more: for they are equal unto the angels; and are the children of God, being the children of the resurrection.

All Angels in the Bible

Summary

Jesus explains that in the resurrection, those who have eternal life will no longer experience death. They will be like the angels and considered sons of God because they are sons of the resurrection. This verse highlights the transformative and eternal nature of resurrected life, where believers will share a heavenly existence free from the limitations of mortal life.

11. Luke 22:43

And there appeared an angel unto him from heaven, strengthening him.

Summary

Having anticipated the crucifixion and the weight of humanity's sins in the Garden of Gethsemane, Jesus is in deep distress as the time rapidly advances. He prays, "Father, if you would take this cup from me! However, not my will, but yours, be done." In response to his prayer, an angel appears to him from heaven to strengthen him.

12. Luke 24:13-23

13 And, behold, two of them went that same day to a village called Emmaus, which was from Jerusalem about threescore furlongs.

14 And they talked together of all these things which had happened.

15 And it came to pass, that, while they communed together and reasoned, Jesus himself drew near, and went with them.

16 But their eyes were holden that they should not know him.

17 And he said unto them, What manner of communications are these that ye have one to another, as ye walk, and are sad?

18 And the one of them, whose name was Cleopas, answering said unto him, Art thou only a stranger in Jerusalem, and hast not known the things which are come to pass there in these days?

19 And he said unto them, What things? And they said unto him, Concerning Jesus of Nazareth, which was a prophet mighty in deed and word before God and all the people:

20 And how the chief priests and our rulers delivered him to be condemned to death, and have crucified him.

21 But we trusted that it had been he which should have redeemed Israel: and beside all this, to day is the third day since these things were done.

22 Yea, and certain women also of our company made us astonished, which were early at the sepulchre;

23 And when they found not his body, they came, saying, that they had also seen a vision of angels, which said that he was alive.

All Angels in the Bible

Summary

Two disciples who were going to Emmaus were joined by Jesus, without being able to recognize him. He came to inquire about the subject of their conversation that made them sad. They told him the story of what had happened with Jesus and how, on the morning of the third day, the women found the tomb empty and met angels announcing his resurrection.

Chapter 19
Angels in the Book of John

1. **John 1:51**

   And he saith unto him, Verily, verily, I say unto you, Hereafter ye shall see heaven open, and the angels of God ascending and descending upon the Son of man.

   Summary

   In response to his testimony of faith, Jesus declares to Nathanael that from this moment, he will see heaven opened and the movement of angels taking place upon the Son of Man.

2. **John 5:4**

   1 After this there was a feast of the Jews; and Jesus went up to Jerusalem.

   2 Now there is at Jerusalem by the sheep market a pool, which is called in the Hebrew tongue Bethesda, having five porches.

   3 In these lay a great multitude of impotent folk, of blind, halt, withered, waiting for the moving of the water.

4 For an angel went down at a certain season into the pool, and troubled the water: whosoever then first after the troubling of the water stepped in was made whole of whatsoever disease he had.

Summary

Having gone up to Jerusalem for the feast, Jesus took the opportunity to go to the pool of Bethesda, where, a large number of sick people were lying waiting under its porticos for the water to be stirred by an angel, who descended there from time to time. For the first one who plunged into the pool after the water had been stirred was healed, whatever his illness.

3. John 12:29

The people therefore, that stood by, and heard it, said that it thundered: others said, An angel spake to him.

Summary

As Jesus spoke to the crowd about his impending death, he was troubled and said, "Father, glorify your name." Then a voice from heaven responds to him in the presence of the crowd, "I have glorified him and I will glorify him again." Some people who heard it said it was thunder, while others said it was an angel who spoke to him.

4. John 20:11-18

11 And seeth two angels in white sitting, the one at the head, and the other at the feet, where the body of Jesus had lain.

12 And seeth two angels in white sitting, the one at the head, and the other at the feet, where the body of Jesus had lain.

13 And they say unto her, Woman, why weepest thou? She saith unto them, Because they have taken away my Lord, and I know not where they have laid him.

14 And when she had thus said, she turned herself back, and saw Jesus standing, and knew not that it was Jesus.

15 Jesus saith unto her, Woman, why weepest thou? whom seekest thou? She, supposing him to be the gardener, saith unto him, Sir, if thou have borne him hence, tell me where thou hast laid him, and I will take him away.

16 Jesus saith unto her, Mary. She turned herself, and saith unto him, Rabboni; which is to say, Master.

17 Jesus saith unto her, Touch me not; for I am not yet ascended to my Father: but go to my brethren, and say unto them, I ascend unto my Father, and your Father; and to my God, and your God.

18 Mary Magdalene came and told the disciples that she had seen the Lord, and that he had spoken these things unto her.

Summary

Despite the departure of the disciples, Peter and the one Jesus loved, whom she had taken to the tomb to observe the apparent disappearance of Jesus' body, Mary Magdalene remains outside the tomb crying. While crying, she bends down and looks inside the tomb. There she sees, sitting where the body of Jesus was, two angels dressed in white. They ask her why she is crying. She tells them it's because she doesn't know where they took Jesus' body. And turning around, she sees a man who she thought was the gardener. This man, who is Jesus himself, asks her in turn, "Woman, why are you crying? Who are you looking for?" And she, not having recognized his voice and still thinking that it is the gardener, begs him to tell her where the body of Jesus is so that she can take care of it. Thereupon, Jesus calls her by name saying, "Mary." At this moment she recognized his voice, turned around, and replied, "Rabboni!" (meaning "Teacher"). She wanted to approach him, but Jesus asks Mary not to touch him because he has not yet ascended to the Father. Instead, he instructs her to go and tell the disciples the news.

Chapter 20
Angels in the Book of Acts

1. **Acts 5:16-20**

   16 There came also a multitude out of the cities round about unto Jerusalem, bringing sick folks, and them which were vexed with unclean spirits: and they were healed every one.

   17 Then the high priest rose up, and all they that were with him, (which is the sect of the Sadducees,) and were filled with indignation,

   18 And laid their hands on the apostles, and put them in the common prison.

   19 But the angel of the Lord by night opened the prison doors, and brought them forth, and said,

   20 Go, stand and speak in the temple to the people all the words of this life.

   Summary

   The apostles gain fame. Crowds of people came from all the towns surrounding Jerusalem, bringing to the apostles their sick and those tormented by unclean spirits. Sick people were even placed in the streets in the hope that, as he passed, the shadow of the apostle Peter could heal them. The apostles healed many people and cast out unclean spirits as Jesus did. Jealous, the high priest and the Sadducees arrested all the apostles and put them in prison. However, an angel of the Lord came to the prison in the night, opened the doors, and brought the apostles out, ordering them to return to the temple where they had been arrested and to continue teaching the people as they had been doing.

2. Acts 6:15

And all that sat in the council, looking stedfastly on him, saw his face as it had been the face of an angel.

Summary

Stephen, one of the seven chosen deacons of the early church, is brought before the Sanhedrin, which is the governing council of Jewish religious leaders. As they judged him, presenting false witnesses against him, they saw him transfigured before their eyes, with his face becoming like that of an angel. Stephen's experience reminds us of the transfiguration of Jesus on the mountain top.

3. Acts 7:30-54

30 And when forty years were expired, there appeared to him in the wilderness of mount Sina an angel of the Lord in a flame of fire in a bush.

31 When Moses saw it, he wondered at the sight: and as he drew near to behold it, the voice of the Lord came unto him,

32 Saying, I am the God of thy fathers, the God of Abraham, and the God of Isaac, and the God of Jacob. Then Moses trembled, and durst not behold.

33 Then said the Lord to him, Put off thy shoes from thy feet: for the place where thou standest is holy ground.

34 I have seen, I have seen the affliction of my people which is in Egypt, and I have heard their groaning, and am come down to deliver them. And now come, I will send thee into Egypt.

35 This Moses whom they refused, saying, Who made thee a ruler and a judge? the same did God send to be a ruler and a deliverer by the hand of the angel which appeared to him in the bush.

36 He brought them out, after that he had shewed wonders and signs in the land of Egypt, and in the Red sea, and in the wilderness forty years.

37 This is that Moses, which said unto the children of Israel, A prophet shall the Lord your God raise up unto you of your brethren, like unto me; him shall ye hear.

38 This is he, that was in the church in the wilderness with the angel which spake to him in the mount Sina, and with our fathers: who received the lively oracles to give unto us:

39 To whom our fathers would not obey, but thrust him from them, and in their hearts turned back again into Egypt,

40 Saying unto Aaron, Make us gods to go before us: for as for this Moses, which brought us out of the land of Egypt, we wot not what is become of him.

41 And they made a calf in those days, and offered sacrifice unto the idol, and rejoiced in the works of their own hands.

42 Then God turned, and gave them up to worship the host of heaven; as it is written in the book of the prophets, O ye house of Israel, have ye offered to me slain beasts and sacrifices by the space of forty years in the wilderness?

43 Yea, ye took up the tabernacle of Moloch, and the star of your god Remphan, figures which ye made to worship them: and I will carry you away beyond Babylon.

44 Our fathers had the tabernacle of witness in the wilderness, as he had appointed, speaking unto Moses, that he should make it according to the fashion that he had seen.

45 Which also our fathers that came after brought in with Jesus into the possession of the Gentiles, whom God drave out before the face of our fathers, unto the days of David;

46 Who found favour before God, and desired to find a tabernacle for the God of Jacob.

47 But Solomon built him an house.

48 Howbeit the most High dwelleth not in temples made with hands; as saith the prophet,

49 Heaven is my throne, and earth is my footstool: what house will ye build me? saith the Lord: or what is the place of my rest?

50 Hath not my hand made all these things?

51 Ye stiffnecked and uncircumcised in heart and ears, ye do always resist the Holy Ghost: as your fathers did, so do ye.

52 Which of the prophets have not your fathers persecuted? and they have slain them which shewed before of the coming of the Just One; of whom ye have been now the betrayers and murderers:

53 Who have received the law by the disposition of angels, and have not kept it.

54 When they heard these things, they were cut to the heart, and they gnashed on him with their teeth.

Summary

During his trial before the Sanhedrin, Stephen was invited by the high priest who presided over the tribunal to speak in his defense. Stephen, filled with the Holy Spirit, opens his mouth and begins to recall the history of the people of Israel from Abraham through Isaac, Jacob, Joseph, Moses, and the crossing of the people in the desert, then Joshua, David, and Solomon and the building of the temple. He reminds the court, among other things:

- How the jealousy of Joseph's brothers led Israel to Egypt and slavery for more than 400 years

- How the people were rebellious even in the presence of the angel who had called Moses in the burning bush to deliver them in Egypt and who had accompanied them on their journey in the desert

- How they gave themselves over to idolatry in the very presence of the Ark of the Covenant, which represented God in their midst, thus provoking his wrath against them

- How God, for His part, remained faithful by:

  o Maintaining His presence among them through the Ark of the Covenant

  o Driving out the nations that occupied the territory and establishing them in the land of Canaan as He had promised

  o Arousing in the heart of David the desire to build Him a temple

  o Allowing Solomon to do so in order to perpetuate his presence among them

Stephen reminds them that they are no different from their ancestors who had killed the prophets who announced the coming of Jesus, and that they themselves killed Jesus. While they judge and kill people because they do not observe the law, which they received according to the commandments of angels, they themselves do not observe it. Hearing these words, instead of coming to their senses and becoming aware, they instead became more and more furious with Stephen to the point of stoning him.

4. Acts 8:26-28

26 And the angel of the Lord spake unto Philip, saying, Arise, and go toward the south unto the way that goeth down from Jerusalem unto Gaza, which is desert.

27 And he arose and went: and, behold, a man of Ethiopia, an eunuch of great authority under Candace queen of the Ethiopians, who had the charge of all her treasure, and had come to Jerusalem for to worship,

28 Was returning, and sitting in his chariot read Esaias the prophet.

Summary

An angel of the Lord speaks to Philip and asks him to go into the desert on the road from Jerusalem to Gaza. Without asking him any questions, Philip obeys him and sets off. Once there, he couldn't help but see this impressive procession passing through the place. The Holy Spirit told him to move toward the convoy. As he moves forward, he will hear the eunuch, current finance minister of Candace, queen of Ethiopia, reading the book of Isaiah while returning home from Jerusalem, where he had come to worship. Philip will take the opportunity to announce the gospel of Jesus to him.

5. **Acts 10:1-8**

1 There was a certain man in Caesarea called Cornelius, a centurion of the band called the Italian band,

2 A devout man, and one that feared God with all his house, which gave much alms to the people, and prayed to God always.

3 He saw in a vision evidently about the ninth hour of the day an angel of God coming in to him, and saying unto him, Cornelius.

4 And when he looked on him, he was afraid, and said, What is it, Lord? And he said unto him, Thy prayers and thine alms are come up for a memorial before God.

5 And now send men to Joppa, and call for one Simon, whose surname is Peter:

6 He lodgeth with one Simon a tanner, whose house is by the sea side: he shall tell thee what thou oughtest to do.

7 And when the angel which spake unto Cornelius was departed, he called two of his household servants, and a devout soldier of them that waited on him continually;

8 And when he had declared all these things unto them, he sent them to Joppa.

Summary

Cornelius, a Roman centurion, was a pious and God-fearing man. He prayed continually and gave much alms among the people. His devotion even impacted his entire household, including his personal guard and his friends. And he was recognized by the Jewish nation for these qualities.

One day, while he was praying around the ninth hour (3:00 p.m.), he was visited by an angel sent expressly by God to:

- Inform him that his prayers, his actions, and his devotion have caught the attention of God

- Send men to Joppa to bring the apostle Peter himself to his house while indicating Peter's exact location

Cornelius obeys the angel's order and forms a delegation of three people made up of two of his servants and a fervent soldier from his close guard. He sends them to Joppa to find Peter, who will come to announce the good news of the gospel to his entire household and to his friends whom he had invited to his home for the occasion. This confirms Jesus' teaching in John 14:6, where He said that He is THE ONLY way to the Father. This text shows that God is faithful to his word and that He does not make concessions or acceptance for people. He will not violate his principles for anyone, whatever their level of devotion or the number and quality of their actions.

6. **Acts 10:22**

   And they said, Cornelius the centurion, a just man, and one that feareth God, and of good report among all the nation of the Jews, was warned from God by an holy angel to send for thee into his house, and to hear words of thee.

   Summary

   Once arriving at the house where Peter was staying in Joppa, the men of Cornelius' delegation explained how an angel had appeared to him while he was in prayer, specifically asking him to bring Peter, who was staying with Simon in Joppa. Peter will follow them to Cornelius as ordered by the Holy Spirit, following the vision he had three times before their arrival.

7. **Acts 11:12-17**

   12 And the Spirit bade me go with them, nothing doubting. Moreover these six brethren accompanied me, and we entered into the man's house:

   13 And he shewed us how he had seen an angel in his house, which stood and said unto him, Send men to Joppa, and call for Simon, whose surname is Peter;

   14 Who shall tell thee words, whereby thou and all thy house shall be saved.

   15 And as I began to speak, the Holy Ghost fell on them, as on us at the beginning.

16 Then remembered I the word of the Lord, how that he said, John indeed baptized with water; but ye shall be baptized with the Holy Ghost.

17 Forasmuch then as God gave them the like gift as he did unto us, who believed on the Lord Jesus Christ; what was I, that I could withstand God?

Summary

Having learned that Peter had gone to Cornelius to tell him the good news, the circumcised friars reproached him. Because, according to Jewish tradition, it is forbidden for a Jew to associate with a foreigner or enter his home. This allowed Peter to share his experience with Cornelius but, above all, to present to the apostles and the believers in Jerusalem the course of events since his visions, which had preceded the arrival of the delegation to him through the visit from the angel to Cornelius to the outpouring of the Holy Spirit on the pagans (Cornelius' family and friends). He concludes by recalling the words of Jesus, who said, "John baptized with water, but you will be baptized with the Holy Spirit" and asking if they can oppose God, who has poured out the Holy Spirit so much more on Jews than on pagans.

8. Acts 12:6-11

6 And, behold, the angel of the Lord came upon him, and a light shined in the prison: and he smote Peter on the side, and raised him up, saying, Arise up quickly. And his chains fell off from his hands.

All Angels in the Bible

7 And, behold, the angel of the Lord came upon him, and a light shined in the prison: and he smote Peter on the side, and raised him up, saying, Arise up quickly. And his chains fell off from his hands.

8 And the angel said unto him, Gird thyself, and bind on thy sandals. And so he did. And he saith unto him, Cast thy garment about thee, and follow me.

9 And he went out, and followed him; and wist not that it was true which was done by the angel; but thought he saw a vision.

10 When they were past the first and the second ward, they came unto the iron gate that leadeth unto the city; which opened to them of his own accord: and they went out, and passed on through one street; and forthwith the angel departed from him.

11 And when Peter was come to himself, he said, Now I know of a surety, that the Lord hath sent his angel, and hath delivered me out of the hand of Herod, and from all the expectation of the people of the Jews.

Summary

Peter was imprisoned by King Herod, who planned to put him on trial after Passover. And as if that wasn't enough, he was chained, placed between two soldiers, with four squads of four soldiers to watch over him and sentries at the prison gate.

While he was sleeping between two soldiers, an angel of the Lord appeared in his cell, woke him up, and ordered him to dress and follow him. The chains fell from his hands, and Peter complied and followed the angel. Together they walked through all the guards to the main door, which opened by itself without any external intervention.

It was only once in the street and after the angel had left that Peter realized he was not in a vision, that everything he had just experienced was real, and that he had just been delivered from the hand of Herod by an angel sent by God.

9. Acts 12:13-16

13 And as Peter knocked at the door of the gate, a damsel came to hearken, named Rhoda.

14 And when she knew Peter's voice, she opened not the gate for gladness, but ran in, and told how Peter stood before the gate.

15 And they said unto her, Thou art mad. But she constantly affirmed that it was even so. Then said they, It is his angel.

16 But Peter continued knocking: and when they had opened the door, and saw him, they were astonished.

Summary

After his miraculous escape from prison, Peter decides to go to Mary, the mother of John, nicknamed Mark. There were many believers who had gathered to pray for Peter. Once there, he knocked on the vestibule door, and Rhoda, the servant, went to open it. Hearing Peter's voice, instead of opening the door, she ran to announce the news to the people who were struggling to believe it, thinking he was an angel who had taken the appearance of Peter.

10. Acts 12:21-23

21 And upon a set day Herod, arrayed in royal apparel, sat upon his throne, and made an oration unto them.

22 And the people gave a shout, saying, It is the voice of a god, and not of a man.

23 And immediately the angel of the Lord smote him, because he gave not God the glory: and he was eaten of worms, and gave up the ghost.

Summary

Sitting on his throne and dressed in his royal clothes, King Herod took advantage of an official event to publicly lecture the inhabitants of Tyre and Sidon, who had come to seek his favor. The people, very impressed and very joyful by Herod's speech, cried out, saying, "The voice of a god and not of a man!" Immediately, an angel of the Lord struck him because he did not give glory to God, and he was devoured by worms and died instantly.

11. Acts 23:8-9

8 For the Sadducees say that there is no resurrection, neither angel, nor spirit: but the Pharisees confess both.

9 And there arose a great cry: and the scribes that were of the Pharisees' part arose, and strove, saying, We find no evil in this man: but if a spirit or an angel hath spoken to him, let us not fight against God.

Summary

Paul is forced to defend himself before the Sanhedrin. Knowing that it was composed of Pharisees and Sadducees, he cried out: "Men and brethren, I am a Pharisee, the son of a Pharisee; it is because of the hope and the resurrection of the dead that I am put under judgment." This statement caused great dissension among the religious leaders present because the Sadducees say that there is no resurrection and that there is neither angel nor spirit, while the Pharisees believe the opposite. Then scribes from the party of the Pharisees began a lively debate, saying that perhaps a spirit or an angel spoke to Paul and that, therefore, he found nothing to reproach him for. The discussion was so heated that he forced the tribune to remove Paul from their midst and take him to the fortress for his safety.

12. Acts 27:21-25

21 But after long abstinence Paul stood forth in the midst of them, and said, Sirs, ye should have hearkened unto me, and not have loosed from Crete, and to have gained this harm and loss.

22 And now I exhort you to be of good cheer: for there shall be no loss of any man's life among you, but of the ship.

23 For there stood by me this night the angel of God, whose I am, and whom I serve,

24 Saying, Fear not, Paul; thou must be brought before Caesar: and, lo, God hath given thee all them that sail with thee.

25 Wherefore, sirs, be of good cheer: for I believe God, that it shall be even as it was told me.

Summary

The soldiers loaded Paul and the other prisoners onto a merchant ship coming from Alexandria and heading for Italy. Surprised on the open sea by a severe storm, the passengers, including the crew, lost all hope of survival after getting rid of the ship's cargo and equipment. It was in this context of total despair, where no one had eaten anything for several days, that Paul stood up to address the people on board the ship. He reminded them of the advice he had given before the ship's departure, which had been ignored, exhorted them to take courage, and reassured them that everyone on board the ship would emerge safely from the journey, even if the ship itself was lost. An angel of God had appeared to him in a dream during the night and confirmed that the lives of everyone on board would be preserved, even when the ship could not be saved.

Chapter 21
Angels in the Book of Romans

1. Romans 8:38-39

38 For I am persuaded, that neither death, nor life, nor angels, nor principalities, nor powers, nor things present, nor things to come,

39 Nor height, nor depth, nor any other creature, shall be able to separate us from the love of God, which is in Christ Jesus our Lord.

Summary

In this passage, Paul brings out the depth of God's love manifested in Jesus Christ. It declares that nothing can separate believers from the love of God in Jesus Christ. By citing some potential sources of separation, such as death, life, angels, dominions, present or future things, powers, height, depth, or any other creature, he makes it clear that nothing can ever deprive or break the bond of love God has for those who are in Jesus Christ.

Chapter 22
Angels in the books of Corinthians

1. **1 Corinthians 4:9**

   For I think that God hath set forth us the apostles last, as it were appointed to death: for we are made a spectacle unto the world, and to angels, and to men.

   Summary

   Paul communicates his intimate thoughts to us in this text where, looking at his journey and that of the other apostles, it seems to him that God has established them as those condemned to death because they are made a spectacle both to the world and to the angels.

2. **1 Corinthians 6:1-4**

   1 Dare any of you, having a matter against another, go to law before the unjust, and not before the saints?

   2 Do ye not know that the saints shall judge the world? and if the world shall be judged by you, are ye unworthy to judge the smallest matters?

3 Know ye not that we shall judge angels? How much more things that pertain to this life?

4 If then ye have judgments of things pertaining to this life, set them to judge who are least esteemed in the church.

Summary

In this passage, Paul wants to remind the Corinthians of the position and supreme authority of the church according to God's vision. He challenges their understanding of judgment and authority within the Christian community by asking them whether they know that we Christians will judge angels. Through this question, he shares that believers will play a role in the final judgment, and even they will judge the angels, which reflects a position of authority. Paul's point is that Christians should be able to resolve their differences and conflicts within the church community rather than turning to secular courts.

3. 1 Corinthians 11:10

For this cause ought the woman to have power on her head because of the angels.

Summary

Paul, here, is pleading for a woman to wear on her head a symbol of man's authority for the sake of the angels.

4. 1 Corinthians 13:1

Though I speak with the tongues of men and of angels, and have not charity, I am become as sounding brass, or a tinkling cymbal.

Summary

The apostle Paul opens this chapter by emphasizing the importance of love. He declares that even though he spoke the tongues of men and those of angels, if he lacked love, he would be like a wind instrument that makes a deafening noise or a clanging cymbal. That is to say, it would be similar to those instruments that make a lot of noise but are hollow inside.

5. 2 Corinthians 11:12-14

12 But what I do, that I will do, that I may cut off occasion from them which desire occasion; that wherein they glory, they may be found even as we.

13 For such are false apostles, deceitful workers, transforming themselves into the apostles of Christ.

14 And no marvel; for Satan himself is transformed into an angel of light.

Summary

Paul shares here that he did not receive any salary in the churches of the regions of Achaia, preferring to receive it from other churches to work in the church of Corinth. He mentions that he will continue to act in this way to remove any pretext from false apostles, from deceptive workers who pass themselves off as apostles. It does not surprise him that they pretend to be something they are not since Satan himself also sometimes pretends to be an angel of light, thus suggesting that these false apostles were influenced by Satan himself.

Chapter 23
Angels in the Book of Galatians

1. **Galatians 1:6-8**

   6 I marvel that ye are so soon removed from him that called you into the grace of Christ unto another gospel:

   7 Which is not another; but there be some that trouble you, and would pervert the gospel of Christ.

   8 But though we, or an angel from heaven, preach any other gospel unto you than that which we have preached unto you, let him be accursed.

   Summary

   Paul expresses astonishment that the believers in the Galatian church were so easily and quickly convinced by false teachings that they turned away from the gospel of Christ. He mentions that there is only one gospel and that those who present false teachings only do so to confuse and try to overthrow the gospel of Jesus Christ. Then he declares that even if he or the other disciples or an angel from heaven come to bring them a teaching that would contradict the gospel they have already received, these people will be placed under the curse of God.

2. Galatians 3:19

Wherefore then serveth the law? It was added because of transgressions, till the seed should come to whom the promise was made; and it was ordained by angels in the hand of a mediator.

Summary

Paul asks a rhetorical question as to why the law was given. He responds by stating that the law was an answer to transgressions until the posterity, to whom the promise was intended, came. He takes the opportunity to indicate that the law was published by angels through a mediator (Moses).

3. Galatians 4:14

And my temptation which was in my flesh ye despised not, nor rejected; but received me as an angel of God, even as Christ Jesus.

Summary

In this passage, Paul rebukes the Galatian believers for abandoning the good news of the gospel and turning away to the law. He takes the time to remind them of the status of sons that they received from God by adoption at the new birth, as well as the zeal and devotion they had shown when he presented himself to them, physically ill, to present to them the good news of the gospel. Paul reminds them that they received him as an angel of God, like Jesus Christ himself.

Chapter 24
Angels in the Book of Colossians

1. **Colossians 2:18-19**

   18 Let no man beguile you of your reward in a voluntary humility and worshipping of angels, intruding into those things which he hath not seen, vainly puffed up by his fleshly mind,

   19 And not holding the Head, from which all the body by joints and bands having nourishment ministered, and knit together, increaseth with the increase of God.

   Summary

   Paul warns the Colossians about people who try to distract them from their ultimate reward. Paul describes them as proud and carnally minded. They hide behind false humility, indulge in angel worship, and meddle in things they have not seen. These people pay no attention to the Head (Jesus), from which the body draws everything it needs to nourish itself and grow through the joints and bonds.

Chapter 25
Angels in the books of Thessalonians

1. **1 Thessalonians 4:15-16**

   15 For this we say unto you by the word of the Lord, that we which are alive and remain unto the coming of the Lord shall not prevent them which are asleep.

   16 For the Lord himself shall descend from heaven with a shout, with the voice of the archangel, and with the trump of God: and the dead in Christ shall rise first:

   Summary

   In this passage, Paul outlines some of the events that will accompany Jesus' return in sequential order. First, He will leave heaven with a cry, the voice of the archangel, and the sound of God's trumpet. Those who have died in Christ will be the first to be resurrected, while those who are still alive and who believe in Christ will be transformed. Together, they will be caught up to meet the Lord in the air. Once with the Lord, believers will remain there forever.

All Angels in the Bible

2. 2 Thessalonians 1:6-8

6 Seeing it is a righteous thing with God to recompense tribulation to them that trouble you;

7 And to you who are troubled rest with us, when the Lord Jesus shall be revealed from heaven with his mighty angels,

8 In flaming fire taking vengeance on them that know not God, and that obey not the gospel of our Lord Jesus Christ:

Summary

Paul is speaking here of the righteousness of God. He mentions that it is right for God to reward with affliction those who trouble or persecute believers. Conversely, to those who are troubled or persecuted and to us, rest will be granted at the revelation of the heavens of the Lord with his mighty angels, in a setting of fire, in order to take vengeance on:

- First, those who do not know God
- Secondly, those who do not obey the gospel of the Lord Jesus Christ

Chapter 26
Angels in the Book of Timothy

1. **1 Timothy 3:14-16**

   14 These things write I unto thee, hoping to come unto thee shortly:

   15 But if I tarry long, that thou mayest know how thou oughtest to behave thyself in the house of God, which is the church of the living God, the pillar and ground of the truth.

   16 And without controversy great is the mystery of godliness: God was manifest in the flesh, justified in the Spirit, seen of angels, preached unto the Gentiles, believed on in the world, received up into glory.

   Summary

   After giving advice to Timothy on how he should behave in the house of God, which is the Church, described as the pillar and the foundation of the truth, Paul presents to him the greatness of the mystery of godliness: God was manifested in the flesh, justified by the Spirit, seen of angels, preached to the Gentiles, believed on in the world, and received into glory.

2. 1 Timothy 5:21

I charge thee before God, and the Lord Jesus Christ, and the elect angels, that thou observe these things without preferring one before another, doing nothing by partiality.

Summary

Paul communicates the responsibility to Timothy—in the presence of God, the Lord Jesus, and the elect angels, playing the role of witnesses—to observe each of his exhortations and recommendations without preference and to do nothing with partiality. It looks like Paul is formalizing Timothy in his position as Minister of the Gospel.

Chapter 27
Angels in the Book of Hebrews

1. **Hebrews 1:1-14**

   1 God, who at sundry times and in divers manners spake in time past unto the fathers by the prophets,

   2 Hath in these last days spoken unto us by his Son, whom he hath appointed heir of all things, by whom also he made the worlds;

   3 Who being the brightness of his glory, and the express image of his person, and upholding all things by the word of his power, when he had by himself purged our sins, sat down on the right hand of the Majesty on high:

   4 Being made so much better than the angels, as he hath by inheritance obtained a more excellent name than they.

   5 For unto which of the angels said he at any time, Thou art my Son, this day have I begotten thee? And again, I will be to him a Father, and he shall be to me a Son?

6 And again, when he bringeth in the firstbegotten into the world, he saith, And let all the angels of God worship him.

7 And of the angels he saith, Who maketh his angels spirits, and his ministers a flame of fire.

8 But unto the Son he saith, Thy throne, O God, is for ever and ever: a sceptre of righteousness is the sceptre of thy kingdom.

9 Thou hast loved righteousness, and hated iniquity; therefore God, even thy God, hath anointed thee with the oil of gladness above thy fellows.

10 And, Thou, Lord, in the beginning hast laid the foundation of the earth; and the heavens are the works of thine hands:

11 They shall perish; but thou remainest; and they all shall wax old as doth a garment;

12 And as a vesture shalt thou fold them up, and they shall be changed: but thou art the same, and thy years shall not fail.

13 But to which of the angels said he at any time, Sit on my right hand, until I make thine enemies thy footstool?

14 Are they not all ministering spirits, sent forth to minister for them who shall be heirs of salvation?

Summary

Without specifying who this book was intended for, the author begins by mentioning that in the past, God communicated with our ancestors on many occasions and in various ways through the prophets. However, in recent times, He has spoken to us through His Son, Jesus Christ, who is described as the heir of all things and through whom He created the world. Jesus, who is the brightness of his glory and the express image of his person, upholds all things by the word of his power when he by himself made the purification of sins and sat down at the right hand of the divine Majesty in the highest places. Having by inheritance obtained a more excellent name than that of the angels, he was made far better than them. Thereupon, the author enters into a comparison between Jesus, the Son, and the angels based on the declarations made by God the Father about the Son, which He never made concerning the angels. Among which we find:

- You are my Son, I have fathered you today.

- I will be a father to him, and he will be a son to me.

- May all the angels of God adore him!

- Your throne, O God, is eternal.

- The scepter of your reign is a scepter of equity.

- You have loved righteousness, and you have hated iniquity; therefore, O God, your God has anointed you with the oil of joy above your equals.

- You, Lord, in the beginning founded the earth, and the heavens are the work of your hands.

- You remain the same, and your years will not end.

- Sit at my right hand, until I make your enemies your footstool.

While regarding the angels, He states:

- That He made them spirits, and his servants a flame of fire

- That they are all spirits in the service of God, sent to be at the service of those who will inherit salvation

2. Hebrews 2:2-9

2 For if the word spoken by angels was stedfast, and every transgression and disobedience received a just recompence of reward;

3 How shall we escape, if we neglect so great salvation; which at the first began to be spoken by the Lord, and was confirmed unto us by them that heard him;

4 God also bearing them witness, both with signs and wonders, and with divers miracles, and gifts of the Holy Ghost, according to his own will?

5 For unto the angels hath he not put in subjection the world to come, whereof we speak.

6 But one in a certain place testified, saying, What is man, that thou art mindful of him? or the son of man that thou visitest him?

7 Thou madest him a little lower than the angels; thou crownedst him with glory and honour, and didst set him over the works of thy hands:

8 Thou hast put all things in subjection under his feet. For in that he put all in subjection under him, he left nothing that is not put under him. But now we see not yet all things put under him.

9 But we see Jesus, who was made a little lower than the angels for the suffering of death, crowned with glory and honour; that he by the grace of God should taste death for every man.

Summary

The author warns against neglecting the salvation that was proclaimed by Jesus and confirmed by those who heard him. God supported their testimony by signs and wonders and various miracles, and by the gifts of the Holy Spirit distributed according to His will. For if the word spoken by angels has had its effect, and if all disobedience has received a just recompense, so those who neglect so great a salvation may expect proportionate consequences from God. The author also specifies that the world to come is not subject to the domination of angels but of men. Is this why someone somewhere had to question God in these words: "What is man, that you remember him, or the son of man, that you care for him?" And he goes on to affirm, "You have made him a little lower than the angels, You have crowned him with glory and honor, You have established him over the work of your hands: You have placed all things under his domination." The author, however, draws attention to the fact that although God has established man over all his work and nothing has been left beyond his control, the reality is totally different. Conversely, we see Jesus, who was made a little lower than the angels because of the suffering of death, crowned with glory and honor, and that, by the grace of God, he tasted death for every man, testifying to the importance of Jesus' sacrifice on the cross for the salvation of humanity.

3. Hebrews 2:16

For verily he took not on him the nature of angels; but he took on him the seed of Abraham.

Summary

In this text, the author explains that Jesus was not interested in helping the angels but rather the posterity or descendants of Abraham. This is why he incarnated as a human being and became fully human, born of the lineage of Abraham, to identify with man in order to save humanity from sin and its consequences.

4. Hebrews 9:5

And over it the cherubims of glory shadowing the mercyseat; of which we cannot now speak particularly.

Summary

In describing the Tabernacle, the author specifies here the presence of cherubim (which are angelic beings). They were positioned inside the Tabernacle in the most holy place above the Ark of the Covenant and covered the mercy seat with their shadow.

5. Hebrews 12:21-24

21 And so terrible was the sight, that Moses said, I exceedingly fear and quake:)

22 But ye are come unto mount Sion, and unto the city of the living God, the heavenly Jerusalem, and to an innumerable company of angels,

23 To the general assembly and church of the firstborn, which are written in heaven, and to God the Judge of all, and to the spirits of just men made perfect,

24 And to Jesus the mediator of the new covenant, and to the blood of sprinkling, that speaketh better things than that of Abel.

Summary

The author presents in this text the contrast between the fathers or ancestors of the children of Israel and the believers. Indeed, when the Lord descended on Mount Sinai, where the mountain was on fire with darkness and storms, the fathers could not approach it, and they were afraid. Even animals could not do so on pain of being stoned. He even mentions the testimony of Moses, who confessed that he was trembling with fear. At the same time, instead of approaching a physical mountain like Mount Sinai, believers came to Mount Zion, which is a spiritual mountain, a celestial city, where they access:

- The city of the living God
- Countless angels
- The general assembly and the church of the firstborn, which are written in heaven
- God, the judge of all
- The spirits of the righteous who have been made perfect
- Jesus, the mediator of the new covenant
- The blood of sprinkling, which speaks better than that of Abel

6. Hebrews 13:2

Be not forgetful to entertain strangers: for thereby some have entertained angels unawares.

Summary

The author insinuates that in our surroundings, there are angels in human guise and recommends that we treat everyone with respect and love and exercise hospitality toward all. For in doing so, we will not miss the opportunity to be welcoming and hospitable to the angels who will manifest themselves to us.

Chapter 28
Angels in the books of Peter

1. **1 Peter 1:10-12**

   10 Of which salvation the prophets have enquired and searched diligently, who prophesied of the grace that should come unto you:

   11 Searching what, or what manner of time the Spirit of Christ which was in them did signify, when it testified beforehand the sufferings of Christ, and the glory that should follow.

   12 Unto whom it was revealed, that not unto themselves, but unto us they did minister the things, which are now reported unto you by them that have preached the gospel unto you with the Holy Ghost sent down from heaven; which things the angels desire to look into.

   Summary

   In these verses, the apostle Peter reveals that the prophets who prophesied about the grace we had received had understood nothing of the details of the prophecies they made about the sufferings of Christ and the glory that was to follow. Although the Spirit of Christ was in them and they had diligently asked and sought, it was revealed to them that these prophecies, which are widely reported today by those who preach the gospel by the Holy Spirit, were intended for us and not for them. Peter also informs us that even the angels would look into these prophecies, and, like the prophets, they too were refused.

2. 1 Peter 3:22

Who is gone into heaven, and is on the right hand of God; angels and authorities and powers being made subject unto him.

Summary

This verse describes how Jesus Christ, after his resurrection, ascended into heaven and now sits at the right hand of God. He also mentions that angels, authorities, and powers were all subject to him.

3. 2 Peter 2:4-11

4 For if God spared not the angels that sinned, but cast them down to hell, and delivered them into chains of darkness, to be reserved unto judgment;

5 And spared not the old world, but saved Noah the eighth person, a preacher of righteousness, bringing in the flood upon the world of the ungodly;

6 And turning the cities of Sodom and Gomorrha into ashes condemned them with an overthrow, making them an ensample unto those that after should live ungodly;

7 And delivered just Lot, vexed with the filthy conversation of the wicked:

8 (For that righteous man dwelling among them, in seeing and hearing, vexed his righteous soul from day to day with their unlawful deeds;)

9 The Lord knoweth how to deliver the godly out of temptations, and to reserve the unjust unto the day of judgment to be punished:

10 But chiefly them that walk after the flesh in the lust of uncleanness, and despise government. Presumptuous are they, selfwilled, they are not afraid to speak evil of dignities.

11 Whereas angels, which are greater in power and might, bring not railing accusation against them before the Lord.

Summary

Peter emphasizes God's intolerance for evil in this passage. No matter where, when, or through what entity it manifests, it will inevitably fall under the judgment of God. On the other hand, the righteous who protect themselves from it have always been protected from its punishment. So, in this text, Peter shows us how:

- The angels who sinned were cast out to hell.
- The old world was destroyed by the flood, while Noah and his family were preserved.
- The cities of Sodom and Gomorrah were reduced to ashes, while Lot was preserved.

He emphasizes that, among the unjust, there is a category that particularly attracts the wrath of God. These are those who walk according to the flesh in a desire for impurity and who despise authority. They are described as presumptuous, willful, and being unafraid to speak ill of dignities. Whereas the angels, who are stronger and more powerful, do not accuse them before the Lord.

Chapter 29
Angels in the Book of Jude

1. **Jude 1:5-9**

    5 I will therefore put you in remembrance, though ye once knew this, how that the Lord, having saved the people out of the land of Egypt, afterward destroyed them that believed not.

    6 And the angels which kept not their first estate, but left their own habitation, he hath reserved in everlasting chains under darkness unto the judgment of the great day.

    7 Even as Sodom and Gomorrha, and the cities about them in like manner, giving themselves over to fornication, and going after strange flesh, are set forth for an example, suffering the vengeance of eternal fire.

    8 Likewise also these filthy dreamers defile the flesh, despise dominion, and speak evil of dignities.

    9 Yet Michael the archangel, when contending with the devil he disputed about the body of Moses, durst not bring against him a railing accusation, but said, The Lord rebuke thee.

All Angels in the Bible

Summary

Jude, in this passage, reminds us how, after the Israelites were delivered from Egypt, some of them were subsequently destroyed in the wilderness because of their unbelief. Likewise, the angels who did not keep their original state but abandoned their home (their glorious body), God imprisoned in eternal chains under darkness, awaiting the great day of judgment. He also takes as an example the cities of Sodom and Gomorrah, as well as other cities like them, which engaged in fornication and sexual relations with other kinds of human beings (the Nephilim). God made examples of them by subjecting them to the vengeance of eternal fire. Jude warns the filthy dreamers who defile the flesh, despise dominion, and speak ill of dignities by reminding them that even the archangel Michael, while disputing with the devil over the body of Moses, had not dared to carry an insulting accusation against him. He only said to him, "May the Lord rebuke you."

Chapter 30
Angels in the Book of Revelation

1. **Revelation 1:1-2**

   1 The Revelation of Jesus Christ, which God gave unto him, to shew unto his servants things which must shortly come to pass; and he sent and signified it by his angel unto his servant John:

   2 Who bare record of the word of God, and of the testimony of Jesus Christ, and of all things that he saw.

   Summary

   The apostle John begins by informing us that the contents of this book are the revelation of Jesus Christ, received from God, which he transmitted to John through his angel for the purpose of showing to his servants the things that will arrive in the near future. And John, for his part, gave an account of the word of God, the testimony of Jesus Christ, and all the things he saw.

2. Revelation 1:19-20

19 Write the things which thou hast seen, and the things which are, and the things which shall be hereafter;

20 The mystery of the seven stars which thou sawest in my right hand, and the seven golden candlesticks. The seven stars are the angels of the seven churches: and the seven candlesticks which thou sawest are the seven churches.

Summary

In this passage, Jesus commands John to write in three specific aspects:

1- On the things he saw
2- On things that are
3- On those who will arrive just after

Then Jesus describes to him the symbolic elements that he saw earlier in his right hand and the seven golden candlesticks. The seven stars represent the angels of the seven churches, while the seven golden candlesticks, for their part, are the seven churches.

3. Revelation 2:1-25

1 Unto the angel of the church of Ephesus write; These things saith he that holdeth the seven stars in his right hand, who walketh in the midst of the seven golden candlesticks;

2 I know thy works, and thy labour, and thy patience, and how thou canst not bear them which

are evil: and thou hast tried them which say they are apostles, and are not, and hast found them liars:

3 And hast borne, and hast patience, and for my name's sake hast laboured, and hast not fainted.

4 Nevertheless I have somewhat against thee, because thou hast left thy first love.

5 Remember therefore from whence thou art fallen, and repent, and do the first works; or else I will come unto thee quickly, and will remove thy candlestick out of his place, except thou repent.

6 But this thou hast, that thou hatest the deeds of the Nicolaitanes, which I also hate.

7 He that hath an ear, let him hear what the Spirit saith unto the churches; To him that overcometh will I give to eat of the tree of life, which is in the midst of the paradise of God.

8 And unto the angel of the church in Smyrna write; These things saith the first and the last, which was dead, and is alive;

9 I know thy works, and tribulation, and poverty, (but thou art rich) and I know the blasphemy of them which say they are Jews, and are not, but are the synagogue of Satan.

10 Fear none of those things which thou shalt suffer: behold, the devil shall cast some of you into prison, that ye may be tried; and ye shall have tribulation ten days: be thou faithful unto death, and I will give thee a crown of life.

11 He that hath an ear, let him hear what the Spirit saith unto the churches; He that overcometh shall not be hurt of the second death.

12 And to the angel of the church in Pergamos write; These things saith he which hath the sharp sword with two edges;

13 I know thy works, and where thou dwellest, even where Satan's seat is: and thou holdest fast my name, and hast not denied my faith, even in those days wherein Antipas was my faithful martyr, who was slain among you, where Satan dwelleth.

14 But I have a few things against thee, because thou hast there them that hold the doctrine of Balaam, who taught Balac to cast a stumblingblock before the children of Israel, to eat things sacrificed unto idols, and to commit fornication.

15 So hast thou also them that hold the doctrine of the Nicolaitanes, which thing I hate.

16 Repent; or else I will come unto thee quickly, and will fight against them with the sword of my mouth.

17 He that hath an ear, let him hear what the Spirit saith unto the churches; To him that overcometh will I give to eat of the hidden manna, and will give him a white stone, and in the stone a new name written, which no man knoweth saving he that receiveth it.

18 And unto the angel of the church in Thyatira write; These things saith the Son of God, who hath

his eyes like unto a flame of fire, and his feet are like fine brass;

19 I know thy works, and charity, and service, and faith, and thy patience, and thy works; and the last to be more than the first.

20 Notwithstanding I have a few things against thee, because thou sufferest that woman Jezebel, which calleth herself a prophetess, to teach and to seduce my servants to commit fornication, and to eat things sacrificed unto idols.

21 And I gave her space to repent of her fornication; and she repented not.

22 Behold, I will cast her into a bed, and them that commit adultery with her into great tribulation, except they repent of their deeds.

23 And I will kill her children with death; and all the churches shall know that I am he which searcheth the reins and hearts: and I will give unto every one of you according to your works.

24 But unto you I say, and unto the rest in Thyatira, as many as have not this doctrine, and which have not known the depths of Satan, as they speak; I will put upon you none other burden.

25 But that which ye have already hold fast till I come.

All Angels in the Bible

Summary

This text presents the message of Jesus Christ sent to the angels (pastors) of the seven churches of Asia Minor.

1- To the angel of the Church of Ephesus, He congratulates him for his hard work, his patience, and his intolerance of evil. On the other hand, He reproaches him for having lost his initial love for Him. Then, He warns him that if he does not repent and return to his first love, He will remove his candlestick in its place.

2- To the angel of the Church of Smyrna, He informs him that he is aware of his tribulations and his poverty (although he is rich) but praises his faithfulness.

He encourages him not to fear the coming persecution by telling him that some members of the church will be thrown into prison. However, He informs him that if he remains faithful until death, he will receive a crown of life.

3- To the angel of the Church of Pergamum, He congratulates him for having held firmly to his name and for not having denied the faith despite the fact that he lives where Satan's headquarters is located. However, He reprimands him for having turned a blind eye to the people who support the doctrine of Balaam and who, for his part, supports those who support the Nicolaitans. Jesus warns them that if they do not repent, He will soon come and fight them with the sword of His mouth.

4- To the angel of the Church of Thyatira, Jesus congratulates him for his charity, his service, his faith, his patience, and his works. However, he reproaches him for allowing Jezebel, who calls herself a prophetess, to teach and seduce her servants to commit fornication and to eat meat sacrificed to idols. Jesus promises to cast her upon a bed and those who commit adultery with her into great tribulation, unless they repent of their deeds, and to put her children to death.

4. Revelation 3:1-16

1 And unto the angel of the church in Sardis write; These things saith he that hath the seven Spirits of God, and the seven stars; I know thy works, that thou hast a name that thou livest, and art dead.

2 Be watchful, and strengthen the things which remain, that are ready to die: for I have not found thy works perfect before God.

3 Remember therefore how thou hast received and heard, and hold fast, and repent. If therefore thou shalt not watch, I will come on thee as a thief, and thou shalt not know what hour I will come upon thee.

4 Thou hast a few names even in Sardis which have not defiled their garments; and they shall walk with me in white: for they are worthy.

5 He that overcometh, the same shall be clothed in white raiment; and I will not blot out his name out

of the book of life, but I will confess his name before my Father, and before his angels.

6 He that hath an ear, let him hear what the Spirit saith unto the churches.

7 And to the angel of the church in Philadelphia write; These things saith he that is holy, he that is true, he that hath the key of David, he that openeth, and no man shutteth; and shutteth, and no man openeth;

8 I know thy works: behold, I have set before thee an open door, and no man can shut it: for thou hast a little strength, and hast kept my word, and hast not denied my name.

9 Behold, I will make them of the synagogue of Satan, which say they are Jews, and are not, but do lie; behold, I will make them to come and worship before thy feet, and to know that I have loved thee.

10 Because thou hast kept the word of my patience, I also will keep thee from the hour of temptation, which shall come upon all the world, to try them that dwell upon the earth.

11 Behold, I come quickly: hold that fast which thou hast, that no man take thy crown.

12 Him that overcometh will I make a pillar in the temple of my God, and he shall go no more out: and I will write upon him the name of my God, and the name of the city of my God, which is new Jerusalem, which cometh down out of heaven from my God: and I will write upon him my new name.

13 He that hath an ear, let him hear what the Spirit saith unto the churches.

14 And unto the angel of the church of the Laodiceans write; These things saith the Amen, the faithful and true witness, the beginning of the creation of God;

15 I know thy works, that thou art neither cold nor hot: I would thou wert cold or hot.

16 So then because thou art lukewarm, and neither cold nor hot, I will spue thee out of my mouth.

Summary

This text continues the message of Jesus Christ sent to the angels (pastors) of the seven churches of Asia Minor.

5- To the angel of the Church of Sardis, Jesus communicates this message:

- The angel has a name indicating that he is alive but, in reality, he is dead.

- Jesus invites him to repent, be vigilant, and strengthen the few people who remain and who are dying.

- Finally, Jesus warns him that if he is not careful, He will surprise him like a thief.

6- To the angel of the Church of Philadelphia, He congratulates him for having kept his word and not denying his name despite the fact that he has little strength. Because of this, He promises to show his love for him by making the people of the synagogue of Satan come and prostrate at his feet, who call themselves Jews and are not. Then Jesus reminds him that He will come soon and urges him to hold on to what he has so that no one takes his crown.

7- To the angel of the Church of Laodicea, Jesus makes him say that He knows that he is neither cold nor hot and that because he is lukewarm, He will vomit him out of his mouth. Then He invites him to resume his communion with Him.

5. **Revelation 5:1-3**

And I saw in the right hand of him that sat on the throne a book written within and on the backside, sealed with seven seals.

2 And I saw a strong angel proclaiming with a loud voice, Who is worthy to open the book, and to loose the seals thereof?

3 And no man in heaven, nor in earth, neither under the earth, was able to open the book, neither to look thereon.

Summary

Here, John sees a book in God's right hand, sealed with seven seals and written both inside and behind. A mighty angel calls out through his voice, which was heard in heaven and on earth and under the earth, for anyone worthy to open the book and break its seals to come forward. And John observes that no one has introduced themselves. He even notes that no one could open the book or look at it.

6. Revelation 5:9-12

9 And they sung a new song, saying, Thou art worthy to take the book, and to open the seals thereof: for thou wast slain, and hast redeemed us to God by thy blood out of every kindred, and tongue, and people, and nation;

10 And hast made us unto our God kings and priests: and we shall reign on the earth.

11 And I beheld, and I heard the voice of many angels round about the throne and the beasts and the elders: and the number of them was ten thousand times ten thousand, and thousands of thousands;

12 Saying with a loud voice, Worthy is the Lamb that was slain to receive power, and riches, and wisdom, and strength, and honour, and glory, and blessing.

Summary

When the lamb took the book, the four living creatures and the twenty-four elders fell down and began to sing a new song of praise. They said, "Worthy are you to take the scroll and to open its seals; for you were slain and have redeemed us for God with your blood from every tribe and tongue and people, and nation; And you have made us kings and priests to our God; and we will reign on the earth." Then John heard, all around the throne of the beasts and of the elders, the voice of many angels whose number was ten thousand times ten thousand, and thousands of thousands.

7. Revelation 7:1-3

1 And after these things I saw four angels standing on the four corners of the earth, holding the four winds of the earth, that the wind should not blow on the earth, nor on the sea, nor on any tree.

2 And I saw another angel ascending from the east, having the seal of the living God: and he cried with a loud voice to the four angels, to whom it was given to hurt the earth and the sea,

3 Saying, Hurt not the earth, neither the sea, nor the trees, till we have sealed the servants of our God in their foreheads.

Summary

In this passage, John sees four angels standing at the four corners of the earth to prevent the four winds from blowing on the earth, on the sea, and on the trees. Then he sees an angel coming from the east having in his hands the seal of the living God and, crying with a loud voice to the four angels, he asks them not to harm the earth, the sea, and the trees until the servants of God are sealed with the mark of God on their foreheads.

8. Revelation 7:9-12

9 After this I beheld, and, lo, a great multitude, which no man could number, of all nations, and kindreds, and people, and tongues, stood before the

throne, and before the Lamb, clothed with white robes, and palms in their hands;

10 And cried with a loud voice, saying, Salvation to our God which sitteth upon the throne, and unto the Lamb.

11 And all the angels stood round about the throne, and about the elders and the four beasts, and fell before the throne on their faces, and worshipped God,

12 Saying, Amen: Blessing, and glory, and wisdom, and thanksgiving, and honour, and power, and might, be unto our God for ever and ever. Amen.

Summary

In this passage, John sees a vast multitude, clothed in white robes and with palm branches in their hands, from every nation, tribe, people, and tongue that no one can number, standing before the throne of God and before the Lamb (Jesus Christ). This multitude cries with a loud voice, saying, "Hail to our God who sits on the throne, and to the Lamb." And all the angels standing around the throne, and around the elders and the four beasts, fell on their faces and worshiped God.

9. Revelation 8:1-13

1 And when he had opened the seventh seal, there was silence in heaven about the space of half an hour.

2 And I saw the seven angels which stood before God; and to them were given seven trumpets.

3 And another angel came and stood at the altar, having a golden censer; and there was given unto him much incense, that he should offer it with the prayers of all saints upon the golden altar which was before the throne.

4 And the smoke of the incense, which came with the prayers of the saints, ascended up before God out of the angel's hand.

5 And the angel took the censer, and filled it with fire of the altar, and cast it into the earth: and there were voices, and thunderings, and lightnings, and an earthquake.

6 And the seven angels which had the seven trumpets prepared themselves to sound.

7 The first angel sounded, and there followed hail and fire mingled with blood, and they were cast upon the earth: and the third part of trees was burnt up, and all green grass was burnt up.

8 And the second angel sounded, and as it were a great mountain burning with fire was cast into the sea: and the third part of the sea became blood;

9 And the third part of the creatures which were in the sea, and had life, died; and the third part of the ships were destroyed.

10 And the third angel sounded, and there fell a great star from heaven, burning as it were a lamp,

and it fell upon the third part of the rivers, and upon the fountains of waters;

11 And the name of the star is called Wormwood: and the third part of the waters became wormwood; and many men died of the waters, because they were made bitter.

12 And the fourth angel sounded, and the third part of the sun was smitten, and the third part of the moon, and the third part of the stars; so as the third part of them was darkened, and the day shone not for a third part of it, and the night likewise.

13 And I beheld, and heard an angel flying through the midst of heaven, saying with a loud voice, Woe, woe, woe, to the inhabiters of the earth by reason of the other voices of the trumpet of the three angels, which are yet to sound!

Summary

The apostle describes in this text the events that take place at the opening of the seventh seal:

1. Half an hour of silence in the sky.

2. Seven trumpets are given to the seven angels who stood before God.

3. Another angel comes with a censer to present as an offering the prayers of all the saints on the golden altar, which is before the throne.

4. Following the offering, he fills the censer with fire from the altar and throws it onto the earth,

causing voices, thunder, lightning, and an earthquake.

5. The seven angels prepare to sound their trumpets.

6. At the sound of the first trumpet, hail and fire mixed with blood are thrown onto the earth. A third of the trees are burned, as well as all the green grass.

7. At the sound of the second trumpet, something like a burning mountain is thrown into the sea, and a third of the sea becomes blood. A third of the ships are destroyed, and a third of the marine animals are dead.

8. At the sound of the third trumpet, a burning star, called Wormwood, falls on a third of the rivers and on the springs of water. A third of the waters become bitter and kill many men.

9. At the sound of the fourth trumpet, a third of the sun, the moon, and the stars become dark. A third of the day and night is no longer lit.

10. John sees an angel who begins to fly in the middle of heaven, warning the earth in these words: "Woe, woe, woe to the inhabitants of the earth, because of the other voices of the trumpet of the three angels, who are still to ring!"

10. Revelation 9:1-18

1 And the fifth angel sounded, and I saw a star fall from heaven unto the earth: and to him was given the key of the bottomless pit.

2 And he opened the bottomless pit; and there arose a smoke out of the pit, as the smoke of a great furnace; and the sun and the air were darkened by reason of the smoke of the pit.

3 And there came out of the smoke locusts upon the earth: and unto them was given power, as the scorpions of the earth have power.

4 And it was commanded them that they should not hurt the grass of the earth, neither any green thing, neither any tree; but only those men which have not the seal of God in their foreheads.

5 And to them it was given that they should not kill them, but that they should be tormented five months: and their torment was as the torment of a scorpion, when he striketh a man.

6 And in those days shall men seek death, and shall not find it; and shall desire to die, and death shall flee from them.

7 And the shapes of the locusts were like unto horses prepared unto battle; and on their heads were as it were crowns like gold, and their faces were as the faces of men.

8 And they had hair as the hair of women, and their teeth were as the teeth of lions.

9 And they had breastplates, as it were breastplates of iron; and the sound of their wings was as the sound of chariots of many horses running to battle.

10 And they had tails like unto scorpions, and there were stings in their tails: and their power was to hurt men five months.

11 And they had a king over them, which is the angel of the bottomless pit, whose name in the Hebrew tongue is Abaddon, but in the Greek tongue hath his name Apollyon.

12 One woe is past; and, behold, there come two woes more hereafter.

13 And the sixth angel sounded, and I heard a voice from the four horns of the golden altar which is before God,

14 Saying to the sixth angel which had the trumpet, Loose the four angels which are bound in the great river Euphrates.

15 And the four angels were loosed, which were prepared for an hour, and a day, and a month, and a year, for to slay the third part of men.

16 And the number of the army of the horsemen were two hundred thousand thousand: and I heard the number of them.

17 And thus I saw the horses in the vision, and them that sat on them, having breastplates of fire, and of jacinth, and brimstone: and the heads of the horses

were as the heads of lions; and out of their mouths issued fire and smoke and brimstone.

18 By these three was the third part of men killed, by the fire, and by the smoke, and by the brimstone, which issued out of their mouths.

Summary

The fifth angel sounds the fifth trumpet; a star falling from heaven to earth receives the key to the abyss and opens it. From there, smoke comes out and obscures the sun and the air. Smoke comes from the locusts on the earth. These grasshoppers have a shape similar to fighting horses; on their heads, it seems that there are golden crowns, their faces are like men's faces, their hair is like women's hair, and their teeth like lion's teeth. They have armor like armor of iron, tails like scorpions, and stings in their tails. The sound of their wings is like the sound of chariots with many horses running into battle. They are given a power similar to scorpions to harm men for five months, especially those who do not have the seal of God on their foreheads. They should not attack green things like grasses or trees. They have a king at their head, who is the angel of the abyss, whose name in Hebrew is Abaddon, and in Greek Apollyon.

When the angel sounds the sixth trumpet, a voice is heard from the four horns of the golden altar that is before God. She commands the sixth angel who has the trumpet to loose the four angels who are bound in the great river Euphrates. These angels are prepared to kill a third of men at a very specific time. They have under their command an army of 200 million horsemen and horses with heads like lions, and from their mouths come fire, smoke, and sulfur. And together, they kill a third of humanity.

11. Revelation 10:1-10

1 And I saw another mighty angel come down from heaven, clothed with a cloud: and a rainbow was upon his head, and his face was as it were the sun, and his feet as pillars of fire:

2 And he had in his hand a little book open: and he set his right foot upon the sea, and his left foot on the earth,

3 And cried with a loud voice, as when a lion roareth: and when he had cried, seven thunders uttered their voices.

4 And when the seven thunders had uttered their voices, I was about to write: and I heard a voice from heaven saying unto me, Seal up those things which the seven thunders uttered, and write them not.

5 And the angel which I saw stand upon the sea and upon the earth lifted up his hand to heaven,

6 And sware by him that liveth for ever and ever, who created heaven, and the things that therein are, and the earth, and the things that therein are, and the sea, and the things which are therein, that there should be time no longer:

7 But in the days of the voice of the seventh angel, when he shall begin to sound, the mystery of God should be finished, as he hath declared to his servants the prophets.

8 And the voice which I heard from heaven spake unto me again, and said, Go and take the little book which is open in the hand of the angel which standeth upon the sea and upon the earth.

9 And I went unto the angel, and said unto him, Give me the little book. And he said unto me, Take it, and eat it up; and it shall make thy belly bitter, but it shall be in thy mouth sweet as honey.

10 And I took the little book out of the angel's hand, and ate it up; and it was in my mouth sweet as honey: and as soon as I had eaten it, my belly was bitter.

Summary

In this passage, John describes an angel who came down from heaven in a cloud, having a rainbow on his head, his face shining like the sun, and his feet like pillars of fire. With a small book in hand, he stood with his right foot on the sea and his left foot on the land. He cried with a loud voice, and seven thunders uttered their voices. As John was about to write down what the thunders were saying, a voice ordered him not to do it but to keep it to himself. The angel raised his hand to heaven and swore by him who lives forever and ever that there would be no more time. For in the days when the seventh angel begins to sound his trumpet, the mystery of

God will come to an end as it was spoken to the prophets. The voice orders him to take the little book from the angel's hand. As he asked the angel for the little book, he ordered him to take it and eat it. As soon as he began to eat the book, John noticed that it was sweet as honey in his mouth and bitter in his stomach.

12. Revelation 11:1-14

1 And there was given me a reed like unto a rod: and the angel stood, saying, Rise, and measure the temple of God, and the altar, and them that worship therein.

2 But the court which is without the temple leave out, and measure it not; for it is given unto the Gentiles: and the holy city shall they tread under foot forty and two months.

3 And I will give power unto my two witnesses, and they shall prophesy a thousand two hundred and threescore days, clothed in sackcloth.

4 These are the two olive trees, and the two candlesticks standing before the God of the earth.

5 And if any man will hurt them, fire proceedeth out of their mouth, and devoureth their enemies: and if any man will hurt them, he must in this manner be killed.

6 These have power to shut heaven, that it rain not in the days of their prophecy: and have power over waters to turn them to blood, and to smite the earth with all plagues, as often as they will.

7 And when they shall have finished their testimony, the beast that ascendeth out of the bottomless pit shall make war against them, and shall overcome them, and kill them.

8 And their dead bodies shall lie in the street of the great city, which spiritually is called Sodom and Egypt, where also our Lord was crucified.

9 And they of the people and kindreds and tongues and nations shall see their dead bodies three days and an half, and shall not suffer their dead bodies to be put in graves.

10 And they that dwell upon the earth shall rejoice over them, and make merry, and shall send gifts one to another; because these two prophets tormented them that dwelt on the earth.

11 And after three days and an half the spirit of life from God entered into them, and they stood upon their feet; and great fear fell upon them which saw them.

12 And they heard a great voice from heaven saying unto them, Come up hither. And they ascended up to heaven in a cloud; and their enemies beheld them.

13 And the same hour was there a great earthquake, and the tenth part of the city fell, and in the earthquake were slain of men seven thousand: and the remnant were affrighted, and gave glory to the God of heaven.

14 The second woe is past; and, behold, the third woe cometh quickly.

Summary

In this text, an angel explains to John the events which will precede the sounding of the seventh trumpet by the seventh angel. Presenting him with a reed like a rod, the angel asks him to measure the temple of God, the altar, and those who worshiped there but to leave the outer court, which has been given to the pagans who will trample it underfoot for forty-two months. Then power is given to the two witnesses, represented before God by two olive trees and two candlesticks, clothed in sackcloth, and they will prophesy for one thousand two hundred and sixty days. During this period, no one can harm them because they can bring out fire from their mouths, control rain and waters, and strike the earth with all kinds of plagues as they please. When they have completed their mission, the beast will come from the abyss and kill them, leaving their bodies in the city square, which is spiritually called Sodom and Egypt, where the Lord also was crucified. Their bodies will be left like this for three and a half days in view of the nations who will rejoice and send gifts to one another because these two prophets had tormented them. When the three and a half days are completed, they will rise again in the sight of all, and great fear will fall upon those who saw them. A loud voice from heaven will command them to ascend, and they will be caught up in a cloud in the sight of all. At the same time, a great earthquake will strike a tenth of the city, and seven thousand men will be killed. The rest, being afraid, will give glory to the God of heaven. And the angel calls this episode "the second woe."

13. Revelation 11:15-19

15 And the seventh angel sounded; and there were great voices in heaven, saying, The kingdoms of this world are become the kingdoms of our Lord, and of his Christ; and he shall reign for ever and ever.

16 And the four and twenty elders, which sat before God on their seats, fell upon their faces, and worshipped God,

17 Saying, We give thee thanks, O Lord God Almighty, which art, and wast, and art to come; because thou hast taken to thee thy great power, and hast reigned.

18 And the nations were angry, and thy wrath is come, and the time of the dead, that they should be judged, and that thou shouldest give reward unto thy servants the prophets, and to the saints, and them that fear thy name, small and great; and shouldest destroy them which destroy the earth.

19 And the temple of God was opened in heaven, and there was seen in his temple the ark of his testament: and there were lightnings, and voices, and thunderings, and an earthquake, and great hail.

All Angels in the Bible

Summary

At the sound of the seventh angel's trumpet, great voices are heard in heaven saying, "The kingdoms of this world have become the kingdoms of our Lord and of his Christ; and he will reign forever and ever." The twenty-four elders, sitting before God, fell on their faces and worshiped God and said, "We thank you, Lord God Almighty, who is and who was and who is to come; because you have taken your great power and you reigned. And the nations were angry, and your wrath came, and the time of the dead, that they might be judged, and that you would give a reward to your servants the prophets, and to the saints, and to those who fear your name, both small and great; and you should destroy those who destroy the earth." Then John tells us that the temple of God was opened in heaven, and the ark of the testament of God could be seen in the temple. There were lightnings, and voices, and thunderings, and an earthquake, and great hail.

14. Revelation 12:7-9

7 And there was war in heaven: Michael and his angels fought against the dragon; and the dragon fought and his angels,

8 And prevailed not; neither was their place found any more in heaven.

9 And the great dragon was cast out, that old serpent, called the Devil, and Satan, which deceiveth the whole world: he was cast out into the earth, and his angels were cast out with him.

Summary

John tells us of a war that broke out in heaven. On one side there is the archangel Michael and his angels, and on the other there is the dragon accompanied by his angels. The dragon is identified as the ancient serpent, the devil, and Satan, who has deceived the whole world. Defeated, the dragon and his angels can no longer remain in heaven, so they are cast out and thrown to the earth.

15. Revelation 14:6-13

6 And I saw another angel fly in the midst of heaven, having the everlasting gospel to preach unto them that dwell on the earth, and to every nation, and kindred, and tongue, and people,

7 Saying with a loud voice, Fear God, and give glory to him; for the hour of his judgment is come: and worship him that made heaven, and earth, and the sea, and the fountains of waters.

8 And there followed another angel, saying, Babylon is fallen, is fallen, that great city, because she made all nations drink of the wine of the wrath of her fornication.

9 And the third angel followed them, saying with a loud voice, If any man worship the beast and his image, and receive his mark in his forehead, or in his hand,

10 The same shall drink of the wine of the wrath of God, which is poured out without mixture into the cup of his indignation; and he shall be tormented

with fire and brimstone in the presence of the holy angels, and in the presence of the Lamb:

11 And the smoke of their torment ascendeth up for ever and ever: and they have no rest day nor night, who worship the beast and his image, and whosoever receiveth the mark of his name.

12 Here is the patience of the saints: here are they that keep the commandments of God, and the faith of Jesus.

13 And I heard a voice from heaven saying unto me, Write, Blessed are the dead which die in the Lord from henceforth: Yea, saith the Spirit, that they may rest from their labours; and their works do follow them.

Summary

In this passage, John tells us about three angels. The first flies in the midst of heaven with the everlasting gospel to proclaim to those who dwell on the earth—to every nation, tribe, tongue, and people. In a loud voice, he exhorted them to fear God and give glory to him and invited them to worship him who made heaven, earth, sea, and springs of waters. The second angel followed and said, "Babylon is fallen, is fallen, that great city, because she has made all nations drink the wine of the wrath of her fornication." The third angel followed them and issued, in a loud voice, a warning against worshiping the beast and his image and receiving his mark on his forehead or in his hand. Violators of this warning risk drinking the wine of God's wrath, poured unmixed into the cup of his indignation. They will be tormented with fire and brimstone in the presence of the holy angels and in the presence of the Lamb and will not rest day or night.

16. Revelation 14:14-20

14 And I looked, and behold a white cloud, and upon the cloud one sat like unto the Son of man, having on his head a golden crown, and in his hand a sharp sickle.

15 And another angel came out of the temple, crying with a loud voice to him that sat on the cloud, Thrust in thy sickle, and reap: for the time is come for thee to reap; for the harvest of the earth is ripe.

16 And he that sat on the cloud thrust in his sickle on the earth; and the earth was reaped.

17 And another angel came out of the temple which is in heaven, he also having a sharp sickle.

18 And another angel came out from the altar, which had power over fire; and cried with a loud cry to him that had the sharp sickle, saying, Thrust in thy sharp sickle, and gather the clusters of the vine of the earth; for her grapes are fully ripe.

19 And the angel thrust in his sickle into the earth, and gathered the vine of the earth, and cast it into the great winepress of the wrath of God.

20 And the winepress was trodden without the city, and blood came out of the winepress, even unto the horse bridles, by the space of a thousand and six hundred furlongs.

Summary

John sees a white cloud and someone like the Son of Man sitting on it with a golden crown on his head and a sharp sickle in his hand. Then he sees an angel come out of the temple, crying to the one sitting on the cloud, "Throw out your sickle, and reap; for the time has come for you to reap; for the harvest of the earth is ripe." Then another angel comes out of the temple in heaven, also with a sharp sickle in his hand. A third angel comes out of the altar, having power over fire, and calls the one who had the sharp sickle to pluck the clusters of vines from the earth that are fully ripe. The angel thrusts forth his sickle, harvests the vine of the earth, and casts it into the great winepress of the wrath of God.

17. Revelation 15:1-8

1 And I saw another sign in heaven, great and marvellous, seven angels having the seven last plagues; for in them is filled up the wrath of God.

2 And I saw as it were a sea of glass mingled with fire: and them that had gotten the victory over the beast, and over his image, and over his mark, and over the number of his name, stand on the sea of glass, having the harps of God.

3 And they sing the song of Moses the servant of God, and the song of the Lamb, saying, Great and marvellous are thy works, Lord God Almighty; just and true are thy ways, thou King of saints.

4 Who shall not fear thee, O Lord, and glorify thy name? for thou only art holy: for all nations shall come and worship before thee; for thy judgments are made manifest.

5 And after that I looked, and, behold, the temple of the tabernacle of the testimony in heaven was opened:

6 And the seven angels came out of the temple, having the seven plagues, clothed in pure and white linen, and having their breasts girded with golden girdles.

7 And one of the four beasts gave unto the seven angels seven golden vials full of the wrath of God, who liveth for ever and ever.

8 And the temple was filled with smoke from the glory of God, and from his power; and no man was able to enter into the temple, till the seven plagues of the seven angels were fulfilled.

Summary

In this text, John describes what he sees. First, he sees the seven angels, filled with the wrath of God, who had the seven last plagues. Then he sees those who had overcome the beast, his image, his mark, and the number of his name. With the harps of God, they celebrated and praised God with the songs of Moses and the Lamb. Then he sees the temple of the tabernacle of the testimony, filled with smoke because of the glory of God and his power, opened in heaven. The seven angels come out, dressed in pure white linen and girdles of gold, carrying the seven plagues. One of the four beasts gives them seven golden vials full of the wrath of God. No one could enter the temple until the seven plagues of the seven angels were fulfilled.

18. Revelation 16:1-21

1 And I heard a great voice out of the temple saying to the seven angels, Go your ways, and pour out the vials of the wrath of God upon the earth.

2 And the first went, and poured out his vial upon the earth; and there fell a noisome and grievous sore upon the men which had the mark of the beast, and upon them which worshipped his image.

3 And the second angel poured out his vial upon the sea; and it became as the blood of a dead man: and every living soul died in the sea.

4 And the third angel poured out his vial upon the rivers and fountains of waters; and they became blood.

5 And I heard the angel of the waters say, Thou art righteous, O Lord, which art, and wast, and shalt be, because thou hast judged thus.

6 For they have shed the blood of saints and prophets, and thou hast given them blood to drink; for they are worthy.

7 And I heard another out of the altar say, Even so, Lord God Almighty, true and righteous are thy judgments.

8 And the fourth angel poured out his vial upon the sun; and power was given unto him to scorch men with fire.

9 And men were scorched with great heat, and blasphemed the name of God, which hath power over these plagues: and they repented not to give him glory.

10 And the fifth angel poured out his vial upon the seat of the beast; and his kingdom was full of darkness; and they gnawed their tongues for pain,

11 And blasphemed the God of heaven because of their pains and their sores, and repented not of their deeds.

12 And the sixth angel poured out his vial upon the great river Euphrates; and the water thereof was dried up, that the way of the kings of the east might be prepared.

13 And I saw three unclean spirits like frogs come out of the mouth of the dragon, and out of the mouth of the beast, and out of the mouth of the false prophet.

14 For they are the spirits of devils, working miracles, which go forth unto the kings of the earth and of the whole world, to gather them to the battle of that great day of God Almighty.

15 Behold, I come as a thief. Blessed is he that watcheth, and keepeth his garments, lest he walk naked, and they see his shame.

16 And he gathered them together into a place called in the Hebrew tongue Armageddon.

17 And the seventh angel poured out his vial into the air; and there came a great voice out of the temple of heaven, from the throne, saying, It is done.

18 And there were voices, and thunders, and lightnings; and there was a great earthquake, such as was not since men were upon the earth, so mighty an earthquake, and so great.

19 And the great city was divided into three parts, and the cities of the nations fell: and great Babylon came in remembrance before God, to give unto her the cup of the wine of the fierceness of his wrath.

20 And every island fled away, and the mountains were not found.

21 And there fell upon men a great hail out of heaven, every stone about the weight of a talent: and men blasphemed God because of the plague of the hail; for the plague thereof was exceeding great.

Summary

John hears a loud voice from the temple commanding the seven angels to pour out the vials of God's wrath on the earth. Thereupon the first angel departs and pours out his vial on the earth, and a noxious plague strikes all men who bear the mark of the beast and worship his image. When the second angel pours out his bowl on the sea, it turns into blood, and every living thing in it dies under the blow. Then the third angel does the same to the rivers and fountains of water, which, in turn, become blood. At this moment, John hears the angel of the waters praising God for His justice in taking vengeance on those who shed the blood of the saints and prophets. The fourth angel comes into action and pours his bowl on the sun, which burns men with fire and great heat. Despite the plagues and the devastation they bring, men do not repent to glorify God. On the contrary, they continue to blaspheme the name of God. Then the fifth angel pours his bowl on the seat of the beast. Darkness and intense pain fill his entire kingdom. But people do not repent of their deeds and blaspheme the God of heaven because of their pains and wounds. By pouring out his bowl, the sixth angel dries up the great river Euphrates in order to prepare the way for the kings of the East. Three demonic spirits, having the power to perform miracles, come out of the mouths of the dragon, the beast, and the false prophet, respectively, and set out to gather the kings of the earth and the whole world for the battle of Armageddon. The seventh angel pours his vial into the air and causes voices, thunder, lightning, a great earthquake of a magnitude never recorded in the history of mankind and large hail weighing each about a talent. Despite the extreme magnitude of the plagues and the devastation they bring, people do not repent and continue to blaspheme God.

19. Revelation 17:1-5

1 And there came one of the seven angels which had the seven vials, and talked with me, saying unto me, Come hither; I will shew unto thee the judgment of the great whore that sitteth upon many waters:

2 With whom the kings of the earth have committed fornication, and the inhabitants of the earth have been made drunk with the wine of her fornication.

3 So he carried me away in the spirit into the wilderness: and I saw a woman sit upon a scarlet coloured beast, full of names of blasphemy, having seven heads and ten horns.

4 And the woman was arrayed in purple and scarlet colour, and decked with gold and precious stones and pearls, having a golden cup in her hand full of abominations and filthiness of her fornication:

5 And upon her forehead was a name written, Mystery, Babylon The Great, The Mother Of Harlots And Abominations Of The Earth.

Summary

John is invited to see the judgment of the great harlot by one of the seven angels who had the seven vials. She is described as having seven heads and ten horns, clothed in purple and scarlet, adorned with gold and precious stones and pearls, holding a golden cup full of the abominations and filthiness of her fornication. She sat on a scarlet beast, full of names of blasphemy, and on its forehead was written Mystery, Babylon the Great, Mother of harlots and abominations of the earth.

20. Revelation 17:7-18

7 And the angel said unto me, Wherefore didst thou marvel? I will tell thee the mystery of the woman, and of the beast that carrieth her, which hath the seven heads and ten horns.

8 The beast that thou sawest was, and is not; and shall ascend out of the bottomless pit, and go into perdition: and they that dwell on the earth shall wonder, whose names were not written in the book of life from the foundation of the world, when they behold the beast that was, and is not, and yet is.

9 And here is the mind which hath wisdom. The seven heads are seven mountains, on which the woman sitteth.

10 And there are seven kings: five are fallen, and one is, and the other is not yet come; and when he cometh, he must continue a short space.

11 And the beast that was, and is not, even he is the eighth, and is of the seven, and goeth into perdition.

12 And the ten horns which thou sawest are ten kings, which have received no kingdom as yet; but receive power as kings one hour with the beast.

All Angels in the Bible

13 These have one mind, and shall give their power and strength unto the beast.

14 These shall make war with the Lamb, and the Lamb shall overcome them: for he is Lord of lords, and King of kings: and they that are with him are called, and chosen, and faithful.

15 And he saith unto me, The waters which thou sawest, where the whore sitteth, are peoples, and multitudes, and nations, and tongues.

16 And the ten horns which thou sawest upon the beast, these shall hate the whore, and shall make her desolate and naked, and shall eat her flesh, and burn her with fire.

17 For God hath put in their hearts to fulfil his will, and to agree, and give their kingdom unto the beast, until the words of God shall be fulfilled.

18 And the woman which thou sawest is that great city, which reigneth over the kings of the earth.

Summary

In these verses, the angel takes the time to explain to John the mystery of the woman and the beast she rides. The angel reveals to him that the seven heads of the beast represent both seven mountains and seven kings who support the woman. Among the seven kings, there are five who have fallen, one who currently reigns, and one who is not yet in power because his reign is yet to come. The angel predicts that the reign of the seventh king will be short-lived. The beast, who had previously reigned among the first six kings, will return to power after the fall of the seventh king to reign as an eighth king before going to perdition.

The ten horns represent ten kings who do not have kingdoms but who will receive one for a short time during the reign of the beast. They will unite with the beast by giving him their power and strength, and, together, they will face the Lamb, who will defeat them. Following their defeat, they will turn against the woman, destroy her, eat her flesh, and burn her with fire.

21. Revelation 18:1-3

1 And after these things I saw another angel come down from heaven, having great power; and the earth was lightened with his glory.

2 And he cried mightily with a strong voice, saying, Babylon the great is fallen, is fallen, and is become the habitation of devils, and the hold of every foul spirit, and a cage of every unclean and hateful bird.

3 For all nations have drunk of the wine of the wrath of her fornication, and the kings of the earth have committed fornication with her, and the merchants of the earth are waxed rich through the abundance of her delicacies.

Summary

In these verses, a powerful angel descending from heaven comes, with a loud and powerful voice, to announce the fall of Babylon, which becomes the home of demons, the refuge of impure spirits, and the cage of every impure and odious bird.

22. Revelation 18:21-24

21 And a mighty angel took up a stone like a great millstone, and cast it into the sea, saying, Thus with violence shall that great city Babylon be thrown down, and shall be found no more at all.

22 And the voice of harpers, and musicians, and of pipers, and trumpeters, shall be heard no more at all in thee; and no craftsman, of whatsoever craft he be, shall be found any more in thee; and the sound of a millstone shall be heard no more at all in thee;

23 And the light of a candle shall shine no more at all in thee; and the voice of the bridegroom and of the bride shall be heard no more at all in thee: for thy merchants were the great men of the earth; for by thy sorceries were all nations deceived.

24 And in her was found the blood of prophets, and of saints, and of all that were slain upon the earth.

Summary

After the announcement of the fall of Babylon, these verses present us with a powerful angel who takes a large stone and throws it into the sea to symbolize the sudden and shattering fall of Babylon. And he announces that no music will be heard in her, no light will shine in her, and no rejoicing will be heard in her anymore. Because she has deceived all nations, and the blood of the prophets and saints and all who were slain on the earth was found in her.

23. Revelation 19:9-10

9 And he saith unto me, Write, Blessed are they which are called unto the marriage supper of the Lamb. And he saith unto me, These are the true sayings of God.

10 And I fell at his feet to worship him. And he said unto me, See thou do it not: I am thy fellowservant, and of thy brethren that have the testimony of Jesus: worship God: for the testimony of Jesus is the spirit of prophecy.

Summary

An angel invites John to write the following words, described by the angel as the true words of God: "Blessed are those who are called to the marriage supper of the Lamb." Hearing these words from the mouth of the angel, John fell at his feet to worship him. But the angel categorically refuses, informing him that he is his fellow servant and orders him to worship God.

24. Revelation 19:17-18

17 And I saw an angel standing in the sun; and he cried with a loud voice, saying to all the fowls that fly in the midst of heaven, Come and gather yourselves together unto the supper of the great God;

18 That ye may eat the flesh of kings, and the flesh of captains, and the flesh of mighty men, and the flesh of horses, and of them that sit on them, and the flesh of all men, both free and bond, both small and great.

Summary

In these verses, John sees an angel standing in the sun, inviting the birds of the air to gather for the "great supper of the great God." The purpose of the gathering is that they may eat the flesh of all those (kings, officers, strong men, and horses, free and slave, small and great) who followed the beast and the kings of the earth after they were overcome by the Lamb.

25. Revelation 20:1-3

1 And I saw an angel come down from heaven, having the key of the bottomless pit and a great chain in his hand.

2 And he laid hold on the dragon, that old serpent, which is the Devil, and Satan, and bound him a thousand years,

3 And cast him into the bottomless pit, and shut him up, and set a seal upon him, that he should deceive the nations no more, till the thousand years should be fulfilled: and after that he must be loosed a little season.

Summary

In this passage, John sees an angel coming down from heaven holding a large key and chain in his hand. This powerful angel seizes the dragon, which is also called the ancient serpent, devil, or Satan, and binds him with the chain for a thousand years. Then Satan is thrown into the abyss, which is then closed and sealed so that he will no longer deceive the nations until the thousand years are completed.

26. Revelation 21:9-10

9 And there came unto me one of the seven angels which had the seven vials full of the seven last plagues, and talked with me, saying, Come hither, I will shew thee the bride, the Lamb's wife.

10 And he carried me away in the spirit to a great and high mountain, and shewed me that great city, the holy Jerusalem, descending out of heaven from God,

11 Having the glory of God: and her light was like unto a stone most precious, even like a jasper stone, clear as crystal;

12 And had a wall great and high, and had twelve gates, and at the gates twelve angels, and names written thereon, which are the names of the twelve tribes of the children of Israel:

13 On the east three gates; on the north three gates; on the south three gates; and on the west three gates.

14 And the wall of the city had twelve foundations, and in them the names of the twelve apostles of the Lamb.

15 And he that talked with me had a golden reed to measure the city, and the gates thereof, and the wall thereof.

16 And the city lieth foursquare, and the length is as large as the breadth: and he measured the city with the reed, twelve thousand furlongs. The length and the breadth and the height of it are equal.

17 And he measured the wall thereof, an hundred and forty and four cubits, according to the measure of a man, that is, of the angel.

18 And the building of the wall of it was of jasper: and the city was pure gold, like unto clear glass.

19 And the foundations of the wall of the city were garnished with all manner of precious stones. The first foundation was jasper; the second, sapphire; the third, a chalcedony; the fourth, an emerald;

20 The fifth, sardonyx; the sixth, sardius; the seventh, chrysolyte; the eighth, beryl; the ninth, a topaz; the tenth, a chrysoprasus; the eleventh, a jacinth; the twelfth, an amethyst.

21 And the twelve gates were twelve pearls: every several gate was of one pearl: and the street of the city was pure gold, as it were transparent glass.

22 And I saw no temple therein: for the Lord God Almighty and the Lamb are the temple of it.

23 And the city had no need of the sun, neither of the moon, to shine in it: for the glory of God did lighten it, and the Lamb is the light thereof.

Summary

In this text, one of the seven angels who had the seven bowls full of the seven last plagues takes John to a great and high mountain to show him the bride of the Lamb. And he showed him, coming down out of heaven from God, the new Jerusalem, the holy city. Then John applies himself to describing the bride, namely the new Jerusalem. Its walls are large and high and it has twelve doors, three in each orientation (north, south, east, and west). Each door is guarded by an angel and bears the name of one of the twelve tribes of the children of Israel. The city did not need the sun or the moon to shine, and when it did, its light was like very precious stones. The walls had twelve foundations, and on each of them was inscribed the name of one of the twelve apostles. The dimensions of the city, such as length, width, and height, are equal and measured twelve thousand stadia, while the wall measured one hundred and forty-four cubits. Its construction was made of jasper. The streets of the city were pure gold, like clear glass. The city was illuminated by the glory of God, and the Lamb was its light. The city does not have any temple because the Lamb is considered to be a temple.

27. Revelation 22:1-10

1 And he shewed me a pure river of water of life, clear as crystal, proceeding out of the throne of God and of the Lamb.

2 In the midst of the street of it, and on either side of the river, was there the tree of life, which bare twelve manner of fruits, and yielded her fruit every month: and the leaves of the tree were for the healing of the nations.

3 And there shall be no more curse: but the throne of God and of the Lamb shall be in it; and his servants shall serve him:

4 And they shall see his face; and his name shall be in their foreheads.

5 And there shall be no night there; and they need no candle, neither light of the sun; for the Lord God giveth them light: and they shall reign for ever and ever.

6 And he said unto me, These sayings are faithful and true: and the Lord God of the holy prophets sent his angel to shew unto his servants the things which must shortly be done.

7 Behold, I come quickly: blessed is he that keepeth the sayings of the prophecy of this book.

8 And I John saw these things, and heard them. And when I had heard and seen, I fell down to worship before the feet of the angel which shewed me these things.

9 Then saith he unto me, See thou do it not: for I am thy fellowservant, and of thy brethren the prophets, and of them which keep the sayings of this book: worship God.

10 And he saith unto me, Seal not the sayings of the prophecy of this book: for the time is at hand.

Summary

In these verses, the angel continues to show John the new Jerusalem. After showing him the river of pure water of life flowing from the throne of God and the Lamb, he shows him the tree of life in the middle of the square and on each side of the river. Then he says to him, "These words are faithful and true; and the Lord, the God of the holy prophets, has sent his angel to show his servants the things that must be done shortly." In response, John prostrates himself at the feet of the angel to worship him. But he categorically forbids it and invites John to worship God. Then he orders him not to seal the prophetic words of the book because the time is near.

28. Revelation 22:16

I Jesus have sent mine angel to testify unto you these things in the churches. I am the root and the offspring of David, and the bright and morning star.

Summary

In the passage, Jesus puts his signature under the writings of John contained in this book and confirms, at the same time, everything that John saw, everything that had been declared to him, as well as all the prophecies that were entrusted to him, which he reported in this book.

Conclusion

The presence and actions of angels represent a fascinating and spiritually significant aspect of the biblical story. From the meetings of Abraham and Lot in the Old Testament to the angelic messages delivered in the New Testament, angels have played a vital role as messengers and servants of God throughout the history of humanity. As we reflect on their appearances and activities, we are reminded of the various intersections between the spiritual realm and our physical world.

While our popular culture often describes angels as ethereal, winged beings, a closer study of Scripture reveals a more complex and diverse depiction. They can appear in luminous, human, or even terrifying forms, depending on the circumstances.

These spiritual beings perform a wide range of functions, from protecting individuals and nations, to transmitting important messages, to leading battles and carrying out divine judgments. Yet they constantly remain discreet, never seeking recognition or adoration.

Studying angels in the Bible is a rewarding endeavor because it provides a better understanding of their purpose and how they operate. This effort is vital not only for those seeking spiritual enlightenment but also for students of theology, Bible teachers, and anyone wishing to delve deeper into the Word of God. The abundance of references and the diversity of angelic activities presented in this work constitute valuable tools for those seeking to unravel the mysteries of these celestial messengers.

By delving into the world of angels, we gain a deeper appreciation of the complex web of interactions between the spiritual and physical. The knowledge we gain helps us distinguish biblical truths from cinematographic fiction and deepens our connection to the divine. With a myriad of angels serving God, their influence continues to extend throughout the ages, leaving us with a sense of wonder at the role they can play in our lives, especially in these end times.

In summary, the study of angels in the Bible offers insight into a mysterious and awe-inspiring realm, always present but often invisible. These spiritual beings bear witness to the richness of God's creation and His continuing interaction with humanity. May the ideas presented in this book inspire you to explore and appreciate the importance of angels in the biblical narrative, thereby enriching your spiritual journey and deepening your understanding of the divine.

If you enjoyed the book, please leave a review on Amazon.

www.ingramcontent.com/pod-product-compliance
Lightning Source LLC
Chambersburg PA
CBHW011521070526
44585CB00022B/2495